CLASSIC INDIAN STORIES • PRATILIPI COMICS

THE LIFE OF BHAGAT SINGH

Published by Westland Books, a division of Nasadiya Technologies Private Limited, in 2025

No. 269/2B, First Floor, 'Irai Arul', Vimalraj Street, Nethaji Nagar, Alapakkam Main Road, Maduravoyal, Chennai 600095

Westland and the Westland logo are the trademarks of Nasadiya Technologies Private Limited, or its affiliates.

ISBN: 9789360455941

10 9 8 7 6 5 4

Comic script: Dr Rajeev Tamhankar, Gaurav Abhyankar
Editorial assistant: Sahar Beg
Art: Sayooj N.P.
Operations lead: Angelin Diana
Quality assurance supervisor: Abhigyan Singh
Art direction: Ashiq Shanavas
Creative producer: Dr Rajeev Tamhankar

Printed at Nutech Print Services Pvt. Ltd

27 SEPTEMBER 1907, BANGA, PUNJAB, BRITISH INDIA.
SOME BIRTHS MARK THE TURNING OF AN AGE. THEY DON'T JUST ADD A NAME TO A FAMILY BUT CARVE A PATH FOR NATIONS TO WALK UPON.
AAAAHH!!
BORN AMIDST THE CRIES OF THE OPPRESSED, A SEED OF RESISTANCE TAKES ROOT, DESTINED TO GROW INTO A STORM.
WAAAN!
HE IS BORN WHO WOULD ONE DAY ROAR LOUDER THAN THE STORM ITSELF.

AS ONE LIFE ENTERS THE WORLD, ANOTHER WALKS FREE—
HIS FATHER, KISHAN SINGH AND UNCLE, SWARAN SINGH, WERE FREED FROM JAIL ON THE DAY OF HIS BIRTH ...
HIS FATHER AND UNCLE ARE RELEASED FROM JAIL. THERE IS NEWS THAT HIS OTHER UNCLE, AJIT SINGH, WILL BE FREED TOO.
BEBBE, HE IS A LUCKY CHILD FOR US.
I WILL CALL HIM BHAGATWALA—THE BLESSED ONE.
THE WORLD, THOUGH, WOULD COME TO KNOW HIM BY ANOTHER NAME—A WARRIOR, A REVOLUTIONARY, A MARTYR ... BHAGAT SINGH.

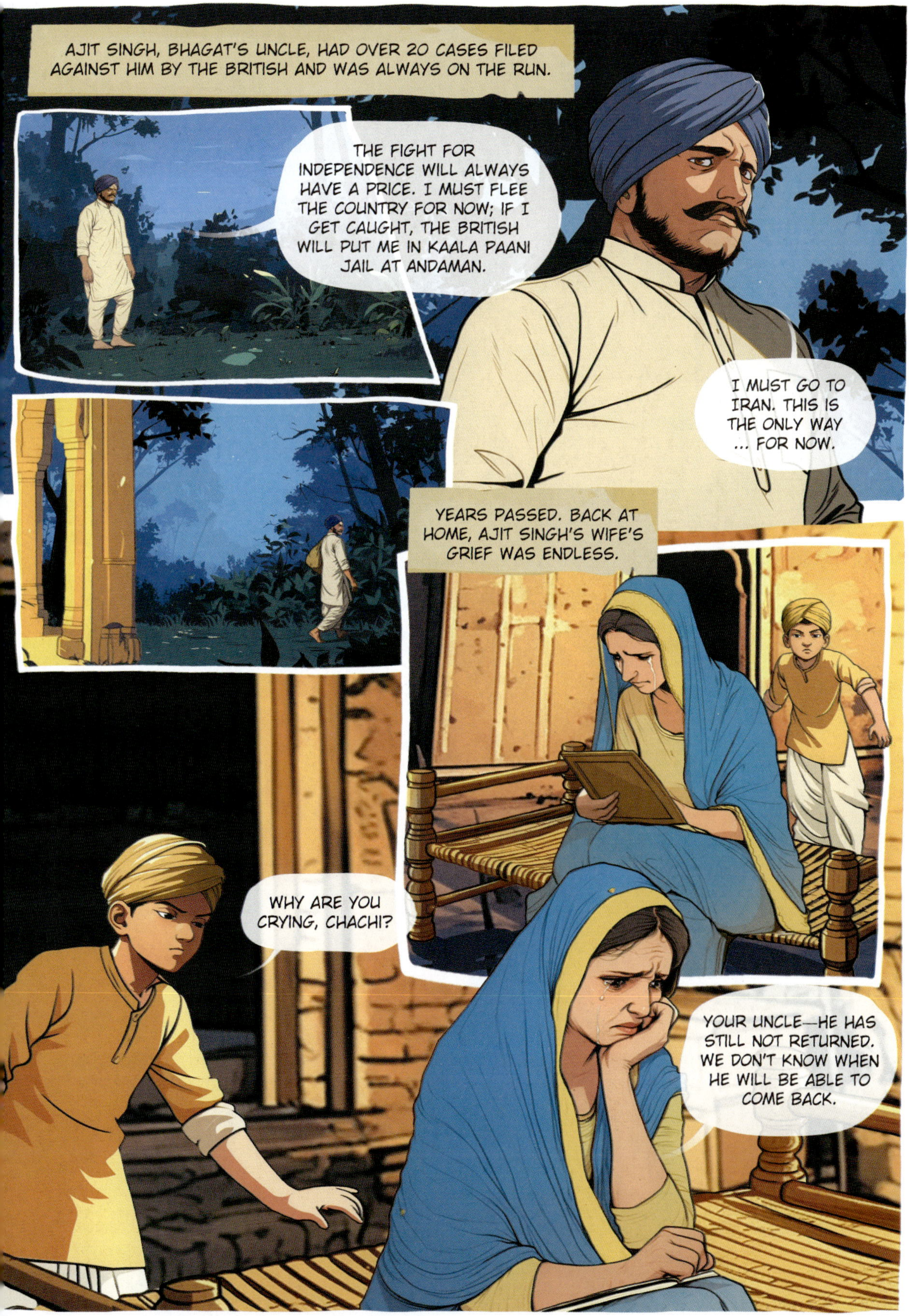
AJIT SINGH, BHAGAT'S UNCLE, HAD OVER 20 CASES FILED AGAINST HIM BY THE BRITISH AND WAS ALWAYS ON THE RUN.
THE FIGHT FOR INDEPENDENCE WILL ALWAYS HAVE A PRICE. I MUST FLEE THE COUNTRY FOR NOW; IF I GET CAUGHT, THE BRITISH WILL PUT ME IN KAALA PAANI JAIL AT ANDAMAN.
I MUST GO TO IRAN. THIS IS THE ONLY WAY ... FOR NOW.
YEARS PASSED. BACK AT HOME, AJIT SINGH'S WIFE'S GRIEF WAS ENDLESS.
WHY ARE YOU CRYING, CHACHI?
YOUR UNCLE—HE HAS STILL NOT RETURNED. WE DON'T KNOW WHEN HE WILL BE ABLE TO COME BACK.

DON'T CRY, CHACHI! UNCLE WILL COME BACK AND WE'LL WIN OUR FREEDOM TOGETHER!
WHEN DID YOU BECOME SUCH A BIG BOY? COMFORTING YOUR AUNT? COME HERE. GIVE ME A HUG!

BHAGAT WAS THE SECOND CHILD AMONG HIS SEVEN SIBLINGS, BORN TO VIDYAVATI AND KISHAN SINGH.
ONE DAY AT THE FARM ...
WHAT ARE YOU DOING, PITA-JI?
I'M PLANTING SEEDS, BHAGAT. ONE DAY, THEY WILL GROW INTO TREES FULL OF FRUIT.
AREY, WHERE ARE YOU RUNNING?
ONE MINUTE, PITA-JI, I HAVE AN IDEA.
WHAT HAPPENED?! WHAT IS THIS, BHAGAT?

JUST LIKE YOU PLANTED SEEDS, I AM PLANTING A GUN. ONE DAY, OUR FARM WILL BE FULL OF GUNS—GUNS FOR OUR FREEDOM FIGHTERS!
MY BOY! I AM SO PROUD OF YOU!
PUTAR, IT'S TIME FOR SCHOOL!
YES MA, I'M COMING!
THERE IS A BRITISH SCHOOL NEARBY THAT YOU COULD ENROLL IN.
NO MA, I AM HAPPY WITH THE ANGLO-VEDIC SCHOOL. I DON'T WANT THE BRITISH TELLING ME WHAT TO LEARN.
OKAY, GO! YOU WILL GET LATE OTHERWISE.
AT SCHOOL, BHAGAT DEVELOPED A DEEP LOVE FOR READING, ESPECIALLY LITERATURE ON FREEDOM AND REVOLUTION.
THESE BOOKS ... THEY TEACH US THE POWER IN FIGHTING FOR WHAT WE BELIEVE IN.
THE WORDS IN HIS BOOKS IGNITED A FIRE IN BHAGAT'S SOUL, BUT IT WAS THE WORLD AROUND HIM THAT BECAME THE TRUE BATTLEFIELD FOR HIS AWAKENING.

13 APRIL 1919, JALLIANWALA BAGH, AMRITSAR, PUNJAB.
THE BRITISH COLONIAL GOVERNMENT PASSED THE ROWLATT ACT, WHICH GIVES THE POLICE POWER TO ARREST ANYONE WITHOUT ANY REASON. THIS IS WRONG! WE CANNOT BE TREATED THIS WAY!
IT WAS A PEACEFUL GATHERING. THERE WERE NO WEAPONS, NO VIOLENCE—ONLY A PLEA FOR JUSTICE.
MA, LOOK AT THAT !
SHHH!
BUT BRIGADIER GENERAL REGINALD DYER, IN CHARGE OF BRITISH FORCES IN THE AREA, SAW THE GATHERING AS A THREAT.

WE WILL SHOW THEM THE CONSEQUENCES OF DEFYING THE BRITISH!
SIR, LOOK AT THEM. THEY ARE UNARMED, THERE'S NO THREAT OF VIOLENCE HERE.
DO I LOOK BLIND TO YOU, YOU FOOLISH INDIAN DOG?! JUST DO WHAT I SAY!
GET IN YOUR POSITIONS AND GET READY TO FIRE.
YES, SIR!

OH NO! THE POLICE!
FIRE!
RUN!!!
ZING ZING ZING!
ZING ZING ZING!
DO NOT LET A SINGLE PERSON ESCAPE.
THE CROWD HAD NO WAY OUT. THE ONLY EXIT WAS BLOCKED BY DYER'S MEN, TRAPPING THE UNARMED CIVILIANS COMPLETELY.

FIRE! DON'T STOP!
OH GOD, PLEASE SAVE US!
THE SHOOTING CONTINUED RELENTLESSLY, WITH DYER'S TROOPS FIRING AT THE CROWD FOR TEN MINUTES STRAIGHT, EVEN AS THE PROTESTERS ATTEMPTED TO FLEE.
WHAT IS GOING ON ...
BANG!
WAHE GURU!
A CHILD'S CRY PIERCED THE SILENCE, MOURNING A LOVE SILENCED FOREVER.
HOLD ON TIGHT, BETA. DON'T WORRY.
MA! WAKE UP, MA!

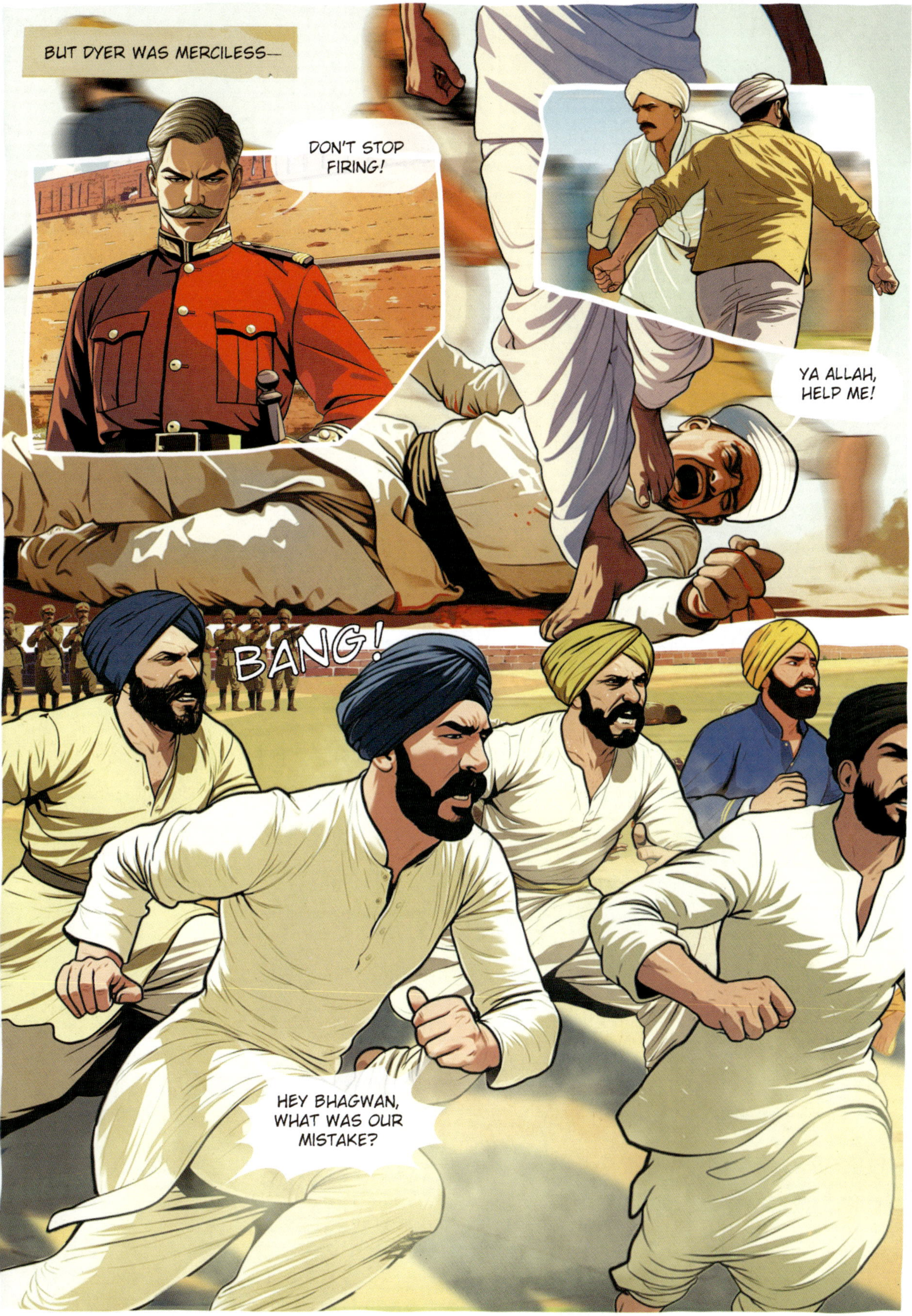
BUT DYER WAS MERCILESS—
DON'T STOP FIRING!
YA ALLAH, HELP ME!
BANG!
HEY BHAGWAN, WHAT WAS OUR MISTAKE?

BACK AT BHAGAT SINGH'S HOME—
KISHAN BHAIYA! KISHAN BHAIYA!
WHAT HAPPENED, PUTTAR?
EVERYONE IS DEAD, BHAIYA.
BUT WHAT HAPPENED?
DYER'S MEN ... THEY CAME TO JALLIANWALA BAGH AND JUST STARTED FIRING. BHAIYA, THEY SPARED NO ONE!
WHEN?
YESTERDAY, BHAIYA-JI. NO ONE'S ALIVE, BHAIYA. NEITHER OLD NOR ...

BHAGAT PUTAR!
WHERE ARE YOU GOING?
PUTAR, STOP!
FUELLED BY RELENTLESS FURY, BHAGAT STORMED THROUGH THE STREETS.
HE RAN FOR KILOMETRES AND EVENTUALLY REACHED THE HORRIFIC SITE.
OH NO!
HEY WAHE GURU! HOW CAN ONE BE SO HEARTLESS!
WHAT ARE THEY DOING TO US ... TO MY PEOPLE?
DYER IS A RAKSHAS!

AT JALLIANWALA BAGH, BHAGAT SINGH WAS FACED WITH A SCENE OF UNIMAGINABLE HORROR. THE BLOOD-SOAKED SOIL, THE LIFELESS BODIES, THE CRIES OF THE WOUNDED—IT WAS MORE THAN ANYONE, MUCH LESS A YOUNG BOY, COULD BEAR.
HOW CAN ANY HUMAN BEING DO THIS?

IS THIS THE PRICE WE HAVE TO PAY FOR OUR FREEDOM?
BHAGAT SINGH LEFT JALLIANWALA BAGH THAT DAY, BUT THE IMAGE OF THE MASSACRE, THE BLOODSHED AND THE INJUSTICE WOULD NEVER LEAVE HIM.
THIS ... THIS IS THE PRICE OF FREEDOM, MY SON.
PITA-JI , DON'T WORRY. I WILL FIGHT THEM.
COME IN, BETA. IT'S GETTING LATE.
THE JALLIANWALA BAGH MASSACRE IGNITED A FLAME IN BHAGAT SINGH'S HEART. HE KNEW WHAT HE HAD TO DO. HE WOULD NO LONGER SIT IDLY.
THE TIME FOR PASSIVE RESISTANCE HAS PASSED. WE MUST FIGHT BACK, NO MATTER THE COST.

LATER, BHAGAT SINGH DISCUSSED THE MOVEMENT AMONG HIS FRIENDS.
WE MUST STRIKE FEAR INTO THEIR HEARTS ... SHOW THEM WE WON'T BACK DOWN.
WE WILL TAKE ACTION. THE TIME FOR WORDS IS OVER. NOW, LET'S DO SOMETHING.
GANDHI-JI IS SUGGESTING A NON-COOPERATION MOVEMENT. LOOK AT THIS NEWS!
The Bombay Chroni
Gandhi Urges Nationwide Boycott of British Goods to gain India's Independence in 1 year!
In a fiery speech delivered today, Mahatma Gandhi called on the masses to boycott British goods and resign from British-run offices, as part of a bold push towards India's self-reliance. Burn their clothes, burn their books! Gandhi declared passionately, In one year, we shall be free! His words resonated deeply with the swelling crowds, sparking renewed hope for independence in the hearts of millions.
THIS IS OUR STAND ... NO MORE BRITISH GOODS!
THIS IS THE FIRE THAT WILL BURN THEIR EMPIRE—LET THEIR SYMBOLS OF OPPRESSION TURN TO ASH!
THE NON-COOPERATION MOVEMENT LASTED FOR MORE THAN A YEAR. BHAGAT AND HIS FRIENDS STOOD UNWAVERING, BURNING BRITISH GOODS AND REFUSING TO YIELD. THEIR RESOLVE GREW STRONGER WITH EVERY PASSING DAY, AS THE FIGHT FOR FREEDOM BURNED BRIGHTER IN THEIR HEARTS.

HOWEVER, ON 5 FEBRUARY 1922 ...
OH NO, LOOK AT THIS NEWS ... GANDHI-JI HAS STOPPED THE NON-COOPERATION MOVEMENT BECAUSE OF THE CHAURI CHAURA INCIDENT.
BUT WHY, PITA-JI? WE ARE NOT FREE YET.
SOME PEOPLE WERE PROTESTING AGAINST BRITISH GOODS. HOWEVER, THE POLICE FELT THREATENED AND OPENED FIRE ON THE PROTESTERS. SOME PEOPLE GOT HURT WHEN THE ANGRY CROWD BURNED DOWN THE POLICE STATION. THREE PROTESTORS AND TWENTY-THREE POLICEMEN DIED IN THAT MASSIVE FIRE.
OH NO! THIS IS VERY DANGEROUS.
BUT WHY SHOULD WE STOP NOW? OUR FIGHT HAS JUST STARTED.
THE FIRE OF RESISTANCE BURNED BRIGHTER IN BHAGAT'S HEART, EVEN AS THE MOVEMENT FALTERED.
FOR HIM, THE FIGHT FOR FREEDOM WAS FAR FROM OVER. IT HAD ONLY JUST BEGUN AND HE WOULD CARRY IT FORWARD, NO MATTER THE COST.
THE STRUGGLE FOR INDIA'S INDEPENDENCE HAD FOUND A NEW FACE—A FACE THAT WOULD NO LONGER WAIT FOR CHANGE, BUT SEIZE IT IN A DARING ... HEIST.

OVER A YEAR LATER ...
THE SETBACK OF THE NON-COOPERATION MOVEMENT SHIFTED BHAGAT SINGH'S BELIEF IN PEACEFUL RESISTANCE. HE TURNED TO BOOKS ON REVOLUTION, HISTORY AND POLITICS.
FREEDOM NEEDS TO BE SEIZED!
COME BHAGAT, WE HAVE TO GO HOME NOW!
BHAGAT, LOOK! WHAT'S GOING ON THERE?
YOU BRITISHERS HAVEN'T PAID US IN SIX MONTHS. WE DEMAND OUR RIGHTFUL WAGES. WE HAVE FAMILIES TO SUPPORT!
YOUR DEMANDS MEAN NOTHING. YOU WILL GET NO WAGES AND NO MERCY. YOU'LL GET ONLY WHAT YOU DESERVE, WHICH IS THIS BEATING!
I CANNOT LET THIS HAPPEN! I WILL TEACH HIM A LESSON.
ARE YOU MAD? INCIDENTS LIKE THESE HAPPEN EVERYDAY! LET'S JUST GO. THIS IS NOT OUR FIGHT.

WHAT DO YOU MEAN, THIS IS NOT OUR FIGHT? EVERY FIGHT AGAINST INJUSTICE IS OUR FIGHT.
BUT WE'RE ALREADY LATE. LET'S JUST GO.
HE'S LEAVING! WE CAN'T STOP HIM. LET'S JUST GO!
THERE WAS NO NEED TO BEAT THE WORKERS. THESE METHODS OF NON-VIOLENCE AREN'T HELPING US. WE MUST DO SOMETHING.

THE NEXT DAY, ON THE WAY TO COLLEGE ...
NON-VIOLENCE IS THE ONLY WAY FORWARD!
BUT WHAT IF THE OPPRESSORS REFUSE TO LISTEN?
NON-VIOLENCE IS ADMIRABLE, BUT EVERY OPPRESSOR FEARS RESISTANCE.
THE BRITISH MASSACRED INNOCENT PEOPLE AT JALLIANWALA BAGH. WILL WE CHANGE THAT WITH PETITIONS?
SO, WHAT DO YOU SUGGEST?
ACTION. SWIFT AND REVOLUTIONARY.
BHAGAT, THAT WAS BOLD, BROTHER! BUT YOU SHOULD BE CAREFUL.
I KNOW, I KNOW! BUT IT'S BETTER TO INSPIRE EVERYONE THAN STAY SILENT.

BHAGAT WAS DEEPLY INFLUENCED BY GLOBAL REVOLUTIONARY MOVEMENTS.
YOU'RE ALWAYS READING, BHAGAT. WHAT IS IT NOW?
LENIN. THE RUSSIAN REVOLUTION TAUGHT US THAT CHANGE DEMANDS SACRIFICE.
HELLO, MR. LENIN.
PLEASE BE QUIET. THIS IS A LIBRARY.
I HEARD YOUR SPEECH, IT WAS GOOD. I'M SUKHDEV THAPAR. THESE ARE MY FRIENDS.
THANK YOU, IT'S NICE TO MEET YOU. MY NAME IS BHAGAT SINGH.
COME WITH ME. I WANT TO SHOW YOU SOMETHING.
WHAT IS IT?

DO YOU WANT TO FIGHT AGAINST THE BRITISH, OR DO YOU JUST WANT TO GIVE SPEECHES?
NO, MY FRIEND. I WANT TO FIGHT.
DO YOU KNOW LALA LAJPAT RAI?
WHO DOESN'T KNOW HIM? HE IS THE CO-FOUNDER OF OUR COLLEGE.
YES, YOU'RE RIGHT! COME WITH ME, WE NEED MORE MEN LIKE YOU.
ARE YOU PLANNING SOMETHING ALREADY?
THIS IS IN OUR MEETING ROOM. NO ONE ELSE COMES HERE.
THE JOURNEY FROM IDEALS TO INSURGENCY IS ABOUT TO BEGIN.
INDEED!

A FEW DAYS LATER, BHAGAT PLAYED THE ROLE OF A REVOLUTIONARY HERO IN A COLLEGE PLAY.
FREEDOM ISN'T GIFTED. IT IS EARNED THROUGH BLOOD AND SWEAT!
CLAP! CLAP! CLAP!
YOU'RE A BORN LEADER, BHAGAT.
LEADERSHIP MEANS NOTHING WITHOUT A CAUSE.
BACKSTAGE ...
LET ME GO MEET SUKHDEV. HE MUST BE WAITING.
BOYS, THIS WAS JUST A PLAY. NOW, WE WILL FORM A GROUP. WE ARE RECRUITING MORE PEOPLE TO JOIN US.
MORE PEOPLE, MORE POWER!
FROM NOW ON, WE WILL BE KNOWN AS THE NAUJAWAN BHARAT SENA. LET'S GET TO WORK!
WHAT ARE WE PLANNING TO DO?
WE WILL SPARK A MOVEMENT.

INQUILAB ZINDABAD! RISE AGAINST BRITISH TYRANNY!
WE WILL RATTLE THE EMPIRE WITH THIS.
NOT JUST RATTLE. WE WILL BREAK IT.
BHAGAT WAS RIGHT! THE TREMORS OF THEIR MOVEMENT WERE BEING FELT. A BRITISH OFFICER PICKED UP A PAMPHLET OUTSIDE THEIR COLLEGE AND WAS FURIOUS.
INQUILAB ZINDABAD! RISE AGAINST BRITISH TYRANNY!
FIND THE SCOUNDRELS SPREADING THIS FILTH!

HUSH! WE NARROWLY ESCAPED. THE POLICE ARE STILL ON HIGH ALERT.
GOOD. THIS MEANS WE'RE MAKING AN IMPACT.
WHAT IMPACT HAVE YOU MADE, BHAGAT?
NO, NO, SIR. NOTHING.
I'M NOT A FOOL. I KNOW STUDENTS LIKE YOU VERY WELL.
GO TO THIS ADDRESS IF YOU REALLY WANT TO MAKE AN IMPACT.
IF THIS IS THE ADDRESS FOR REAL CHANGE, THEN WE ARE HEADING STRAIGHT FOR IT!

WHO IS IT?
I'M SUKHDEV.
GET IN.
I'M BHAGAT.
I AM RAJGURU. IT'S GOOD TO SEE YOU, BHAGAT AND SUKHDEV. DID ANYONE FOLLOW YOU?
NO, NO ONE KNOWS WE ARE HERE.
PLEASE COME IN!
RAMPRASAD BISMIL
CHANDRASHEKHAR AZAD
WELCOME TO THE HINDUSTAN REPUBLICAN ASSOCIATION (HRA)! IF YOU ARE HERE, IT MEANS YOU'VE MADE A CHOICE.

CHANDRASHEKHAR AZAD AND RAMPRASAD BISMIL ARE HERE.
OUR PATH IS DIFFERENT AND NOT EASY.
WE ARE READY TO DO ANYTHING FOR OUR COUNTRY.
A REVOLUTIONARY MUST KNOW HIS TOOLS.
HERE, TAKE THIS! THIS IS YOUR INITIATION.
I'LL USE THESE TOOLS TO WRITE HISTORY.

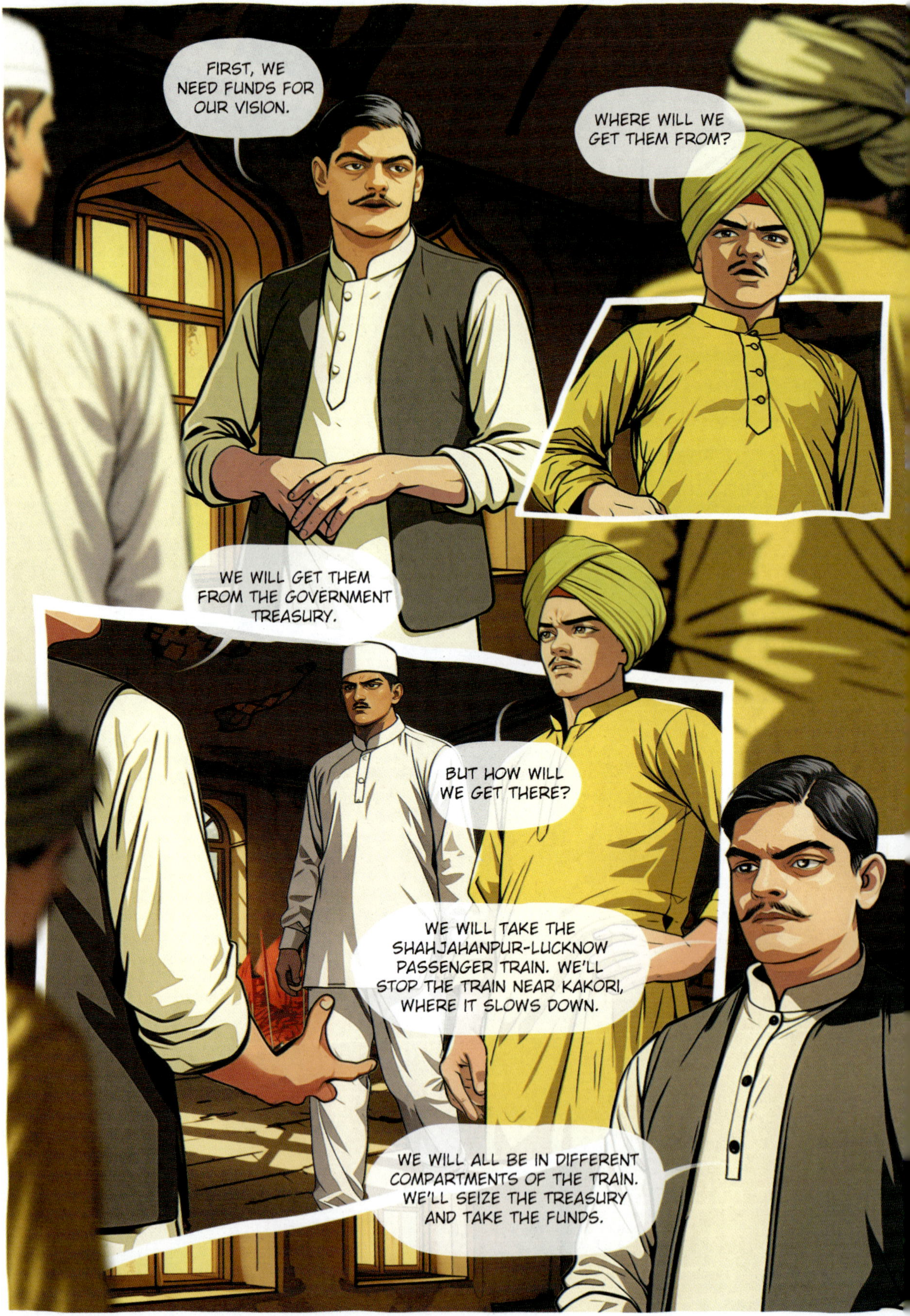
FIRST, WE NEED FUNDS FOR OUR VISION.
WHERE WILL WE GET THEM FROM?
WE WILL GET THEM FROM THE GOVERNMENT TREASURY.
BUT HOW WILL WE GET THERE?
WE WILL TAKE THE SHAHJAHANPUR-LUCKNOW PASSENGER TRAIN. WE'LL STOP THE TRAIN NEAR KAKORI, WHERE IT SLOWS DOWN.
WE WILL ALL BE IN DIFFERENT COMPARTMENTS OF THE TRAIN. WE'LL SEIZE THE TREASURY AND TAKE THE FUNDS.

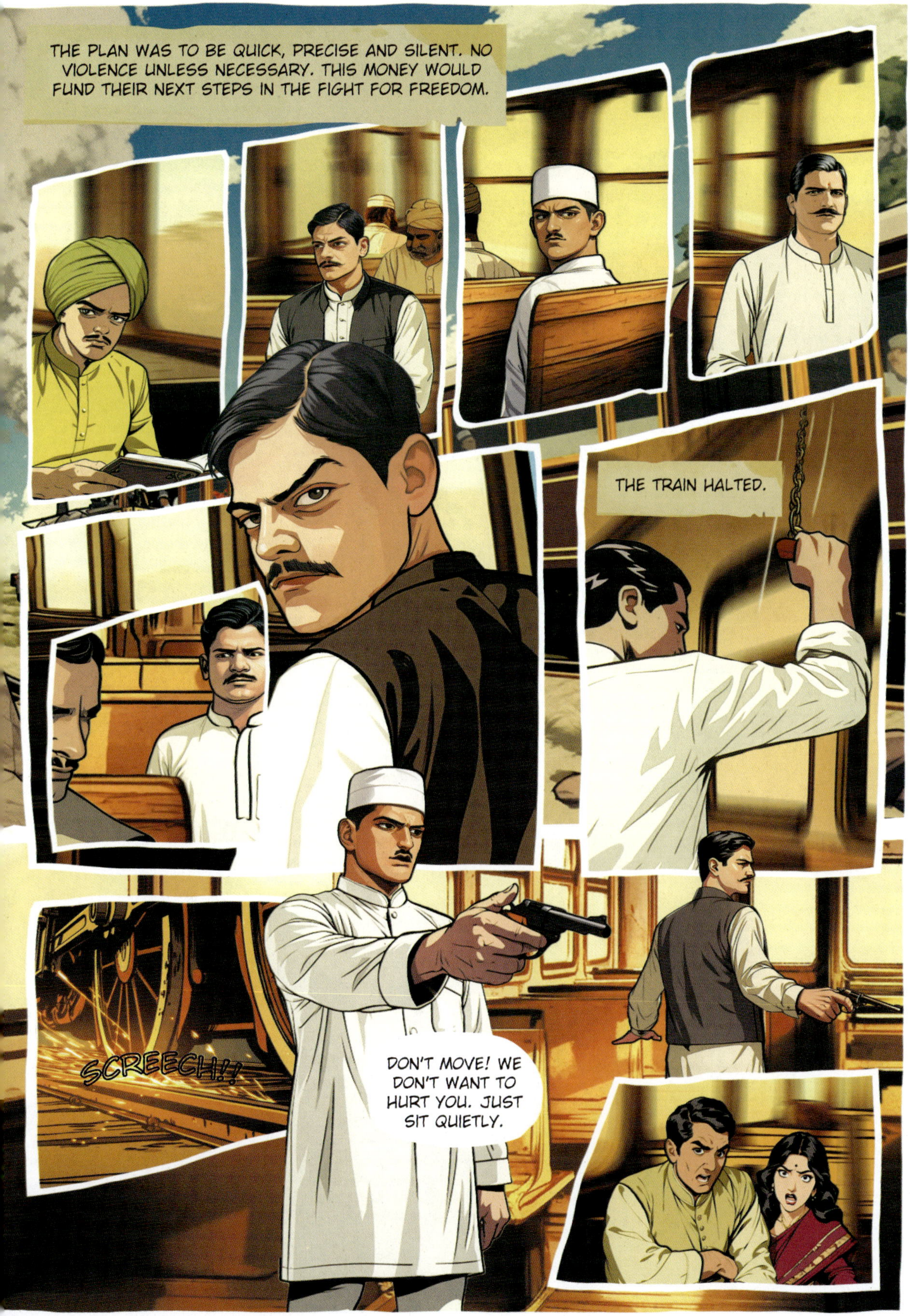
THE PLAN WAS TO BE QUICK, PRECISE AND SILENT. NO VIOLENCE UNLESS NECESSARY. THIS MONEY WOULD FUND THEIR NEXT STEPS IN THE FIGHT FOR FREEDOM.
THE TRAIN HALTED.
SCREECH!!
DON'T MOVE! WE DON'T WANT TO HURT YOU. JUST SIT QUIETLY.

HURRY UP! WE DON'T HAVE MUCH TIME.
LET'S GO! RUN, RUN, RUN!
RUN! RUN!
WHAT HAPPENED?
OH NO! THE TREASURY HAS BEEN ROBBED!

BACK AT THEIR HIDEOUT, BISMIL COMMENDED THE TEAM.
YOU ALL DID GOOD WORK. NOW STAY LOW FOR A WHILE. WE WON'T HOLD MEETINGS FOR A FEW DAYS.
INQLAB ZINDABAD
A FEW DAYS LATER, BHAGAT ADDRESSED HIS NAUJAWAN BHARAT SENA MEMBERS.
BOYS, THE SIMON COMMISSION HAS COME TO INDIA TO STUDY OUR CONSTITUTION, BUT THERE ARE NO INDIANS IN IT.
THIS MEANS THAT THE SIMON COMMISSION WILL ONLY MAKE CHANGES THAT SERVE THEM.
THIS IS WRONG!
YES, THAT'S WHY OUR KING OF PUNJAB, LALA LAJPAT RAI, HAS ORGANISED A PROTEST AGAINST THE SIMON COMMISSION. TOMORROW, WE WILL GO AND SUPPORT HIM.
PREPARE SLOGANS— SIMON GO BACK.

PROTESTERS GATHERED TO OPPOSE THE SIMON COMMISSION IN LAHORE.
SIMON, G BAC
SIMON GO BACK!
WE REJECT THIS COMMISSION. INDIA WILL DECIDE ITS OWN FUTURE!
LALAJI'S WORDS ARE LIGHTING A FIRE.
SIMON GO BACK!
SIMON GO BACK!

J. SCOTT, THE BRITISH POLICE OFFICER IN CHARGE, ORDERED A LATHI CHARGE ON THE PROTESTERS.
CHARGE! NOW!

THERE'S THEIR LEADER! GET HIM!
WE WON'T BACK DOWN!
AAH!
LALA LAJPAT RAI STOOD HIS GROUND, DESPITE BEING HIT WITH A LATHI ON HIS HEAD.
YOU CAN'T SILENCE THE VOICE OF INDIA!

OH? WE WILL SURELY SILENCE THE VOICE.
IN FACT, WE WILL SILENCE EVERY SINGLE VOICE!
LALAJI, STEP BACK!
THIS IS MY FIGHT.
LALAJI! ARE YOU HURT?
THIS WOUND ... IS ... INDIA'S. FIGHT ... FOR ... HER.
THEY'VE CROSSED A LINE, BHAGAT.
WE'LL MAKE THEM PAY.

HOSPITAL
अस्पताल
WE MUST HURRY!
THE SHOTS THAT HIT ME ARE THE LAST NAILS TO THE COFFIN OF BRITISH RULE IN INDIA.
THE DOCTORS AREN'T SAYING ANYTHING. I DON'T THINK HE'LL SURVIVE, BHAGAT.
IT WAS SCOTT WHO ORDERED THE ATTACK. HE MUST FACE JUSTICE.
THIS IS NOT THE TIME TO CRY. IT IS THE TIME FOR ... REVENGE!

IN DECEMBER 1928, LAHORE, THEIR REVENGE PLAN STARTED TO TAKE SHAPE ...
COMRADES, LISTEN!
SCOTT DESERVES TO DIE FOR WHAT HE DID. THOSE MEN BEAT LALAJI TO DEATH. WE LOST HIM BECAUSE OF SCOTT. THAT BASTARDS COTT!
CALM DOWN, RAJGURU. WE NEED TO FOCUS ON THE PLAN.
ONLY SCOTT'S DEATH WILL SEND THEM OUR MESSAGE.
EVERYDAY, SCOTT STEPS OUT AT 4 P.M. FROM THE LAHORE DISTRICT POLICE HEADQUARTERS. THAT'S WHEN WE SHOULD STRIKE.

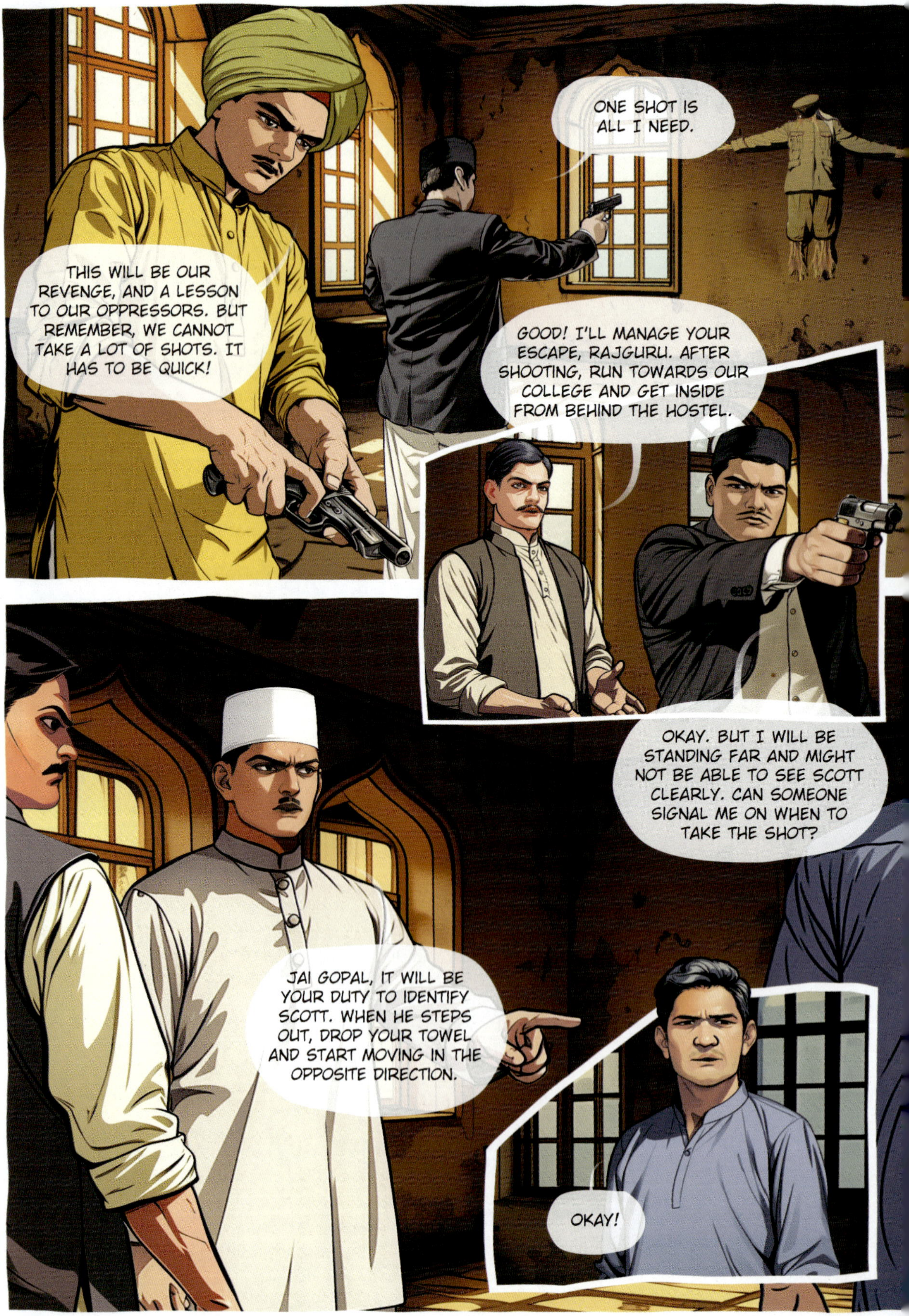
THIS WILL BE OUR REVENGE, AND A LESSON TO OUR OPPRESSORS. BUT REMEMBER, WE CANNOT TAKE A LOT OF SHOTS. IT HAS TO BE QUICK!
ONE SHOT IS ALL I NEED.
GOOD! I'LL MANAGE YOUR ESCAPE, RAJGURU. AFTER SHOOTING, RUN TOWARDS OUR COLLEGE AND GET INSIDE FROM BEHIND THE HOSTEL.
OKAY. BUT I WILL BE STANDING FAR AND MIGHT NOT BE ABLE TO SEE SCOTT CLEARLY. CAN SOMEONE SIGNAL ME ON WHEN TO TAKE THE SHOT?
JAI GOPAL, IT WILL BE YOUR DUTY TO IDENTIFY SCOTT. WHEN HE STEPS OUT, DROP YOUR TOWEL AND START MOVING IN THE OPPOSITE DIRECTION.
OKAY!

REMEMBER COMRADES, IF ANYTHING HAPPENS, THIS ONE IS FOR YOUR LALAJI, YOUR COUNTRY! KOI KISIKA NAM NAHI BATAEGA.
YES, EVEN IF WE HAVE TO DIE, WE WILL NEVER REVEAL ANY NAMES.
LONG LIVE THE REVOLUTION!

17 DECEMBER 1928. THE HOUR ARRIVED.
POLICE STATION LAHORE
HE'S COMING!
WAIT FOR THE SIGNAL.
AS PLANNED, THEY NOTICED JAI GOPAL DROPPING HIS TOWEL ON THE GROUND.
IT'S TIME.
OH, NO NO NO!

WAIT! WAIT! HE'S NOT ...
BANG!
THUPP!

RUN! RUN!
IN A SINGLE MOMENT, THE REVOLUTION CLAIMED ITS FIRST RECKONING—JUSTICE FOR LALA LAJPAT RAI CAME AT THE COST OF BLOODSHED. BUT IT WASN'T SCOTT'S. IT WAS SAUNDERS, WHO HAD BEEN MISTAKEN FOR SCOTT.
BANG!
COME AND CATCH ME, YOU BRITISH DOGS!
THEY STARTED RUNNING TO THE NEIGHBORHOOD DAV COLLEGE.

FIND WHOEVER DID THIS!
WE DON'T WANT TO SHOOT ANY INDIANS! DON'T FOLLOW US!
I AM BOUND TO MY DUTY!
SO AM I!
BANG!

THEY ALL RETURNED TO THEIR HIDEOUT.
DID ANYONE FOLLOW YOU HERE ?
NO. BUT WE'VE MADE A MISTAKE. WE SHOT SAUNDERS!
WHAT?!
I TRIED TO STOP YOU, BUT IT WAS TOO LATE!
OH NO! WHAT HAVE WE DONE!
BUT ...
BOYS! BOYS! DON'T PANIC NOW. SOMEONE HAD TO DIE. SAUNDERS, A BRITISHER, HAS DIED. THAT'S ALL!
WE HAVE TO REMAIN STRONG, OTHERWISE OUR MOVEMENT WILL SUFFER.

THE NEXT DAY ...
THE POLICE ARE SEARCHING EVERYWHERE. I DON'T THINK IT'S SAFE TO STAY HERE.
BUT WHERE WILL WE GO?
YOU SHOULD EAT FIRST. I'VE SENT WORD TO DURGA BHABHI. SHE WILL MANAGE YOUR ESCAPE.
WHO IS SHE?
SHE IS THE WIFE OF THE GREAT REVOLUTIONARY BHAGAWATI CHARAN VOHRA.
BHAGWATI CHARAN VOHRA WAS A CLOSE ASSOCIATE OF BHAGAT SINGH AND THE AUTHOR OF 'THE PHILOSOPHY OF THE BOMB'.

AT DURGA BHABHI'S DOOR ...
COME IN! GET SOME REST FOR NOW. WE WILL LEAVE IN THE MORNING.
THANK YOU FOR HELPING US. WE'LL ALWAYS BE IN YOUR DEBT.
THERE IS NO NEED FOR THAT BHAGAT. JUST REMEMBER, CHANGE THE WAY YOU LOOK BEFORE WE GO.

THE NEXT MORNING.
OH! HAVE YOU GONE MAD?
IS THIS ALLOWED IN SIKHISM? BHAGAT, CUTTING YOUR KES ... IT'S MORE THAN JUST HAIR. IT'S PART OF YOUR FAITH, YOUR IDENTITY.
BHAGAT JUST SMILED SILENTLY.
IT'S JUST HAIR, SUKHDEV. DON'T WORRY, IT WILL GROW BACK.
TAKE THIS COAT AND HAT, IT WILL HIDE YOUR FACE. AND BE CONFIDENT IN FRONT OF POLICE OFFICERS. RAJGURU, YOU'LL DRESS LIKE OUR SERVANT. WEAR THESE CLOTHES.
OKAY, BHABHI.
I HAVE WRITTEN A FEW PAMPHLETS. GIVE THEM TO OUR BOYS AND SPREAD THEM EVERYWHERE. THE MESSAGE IS IMPORTANT. IT SHOULD REACH EVERYONE.
OKAY BHAGAT, BE SAFE. TAKE CARE OF YOURSELF, BROTHER.
DON'T WORRY, WE WILL MEET SOON.

HAVE YOU HEARD? SAUNDERS WAS KILLED BY BHAGAT SINGH'S GROUP!
FINALLY, SOMEONE IS STANDING UP TO THE BRITISH.
Inquilab Zindabad
We don't want to kill anyone, but this was for revenge! We take responsibility for Saunders's murder. The officer was killed because he was a member of a 'wrongful institute'. This is for Lalaji.
Long live the revolution.
Balraj
Commander in Chief
HSRA
18 December 1928
THE REVOLUTIONARY SPIRIT SPREAD LIKE WILDFIRE. BHAGAT SINGH ALWAYS USED THE NAME 'BALRAJ' IN HIS MESSAGES IN PAMPHLETS AND NEWSPAPERS.
THE ATMOSPHERE WAS TENSE AMONGST THE BRITISH OFFICIALS.
THESE MEN ARE WAY MORE DANGEROUS THAN WE THOUGHT.
WE NEED TO DOUBLE THE REWARD FOR THEIR CAPTURE!

MEANWHILE, BHAGAT SINGH, DURGA BHABHI, CHANDRASHEKHAR AZAD AND SHIVRAM RAJGURU HAD ARRIVED AT THE LAHORE RAILWAY STATION.
RADHE RADHE, OFFICER!
YES, RADHE RADHE. GET INSIDE.
TAKE ALL THE BAGS INSIDE CAREFULLY! OTHERWISE, I'LL THROW YOU OUT OF THE TRAIN!
BHAGAT HAS REALLY EMBRACED HIS ROLE AS AN OFFICER.
JI SAHIB, I'LL BE QUICK!
EVERY STEP WE TAKE BRINGS US CLOSER TO THE INEVITABLE.
IN THE SILENCE OF THEIR RESOLVE, TREMORS WERE BREWING—TREMORS THAT WOULD SHAKE THE FOUNDATION OF THE EMPIRE WITH A GIGANTIC ... BLAST!

THEY MET DURGA BHABHI'S HUSBAND, BHAGWATI CHARAN VOHRA, AT THE CALCUTTA RAILWAY STATION.
BHAGAT, I HAVE ARRANGED YOUR STAY AT MY FRIEND'S HOUSE. HERE ARE THE DOCUMENTS OF YOUR NEW IDENTITY.
SO MY NEW NAME IS HARI. THANK YOU FOR YOUR HELP.

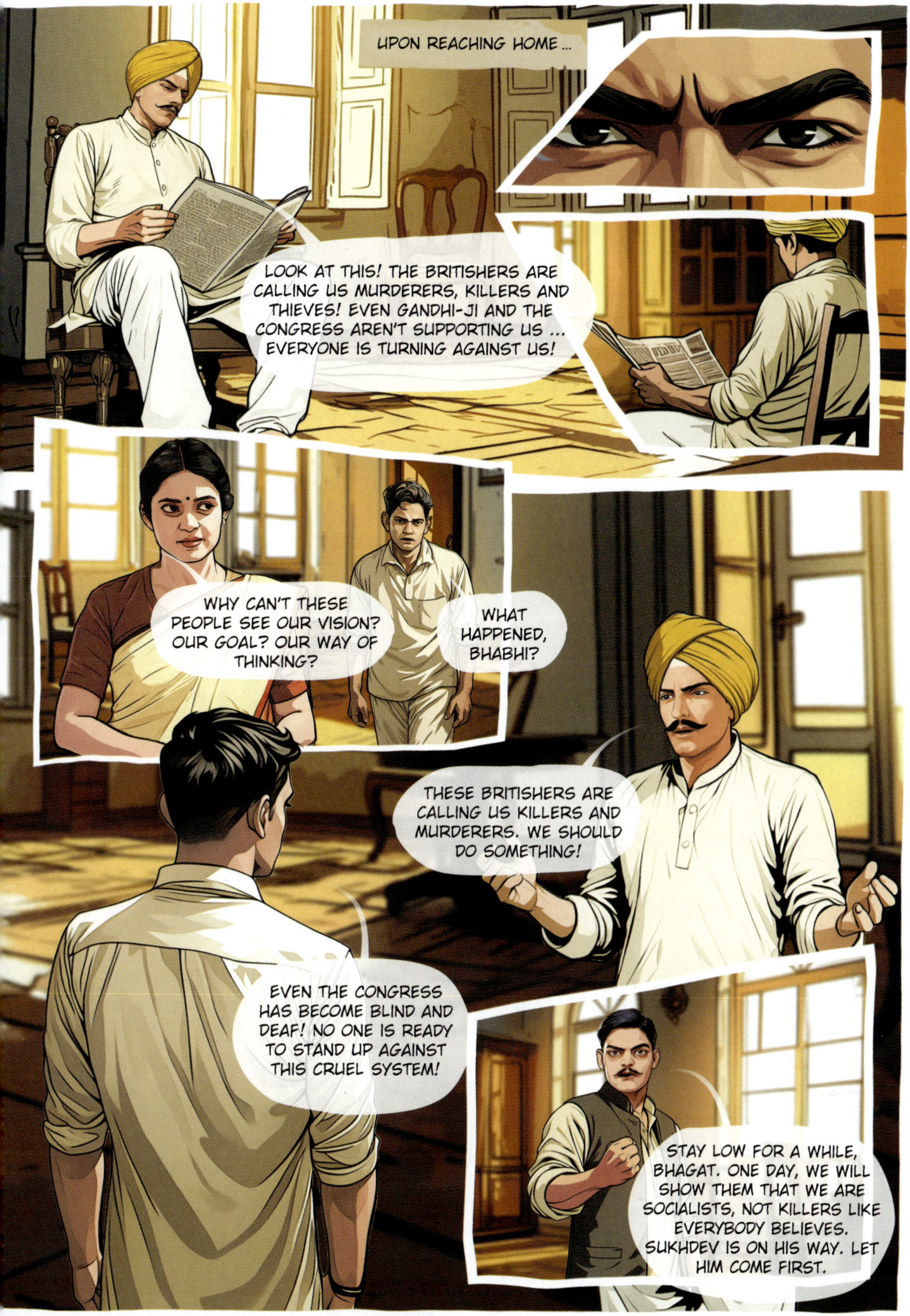

UPON REACHING HOME ...
LOOK AT THIS! THE BRITISHERS ARE CALLING US MURDERERS, KILLERS AND THIEVES! EVEN GANDHI-JI AND THE CONGRESS AREN'T SUPPORTING US ... EVERYONE IS TURNING AGAINST US!
WHY CAN'T THESE PEOPLE SEE OUR VISION? OUR GOAL? OUR WAY OF THINKING?
WHAT HAPPENED, BHABHI?
THESE BRITISHERS ARE CALLING US KILLERS AND MURDERERS. WE SHOULD DO SOMETHING!
EVEN THE CONGRESS HAS BECOME BLIND AND DEAF! NO ONE IS READY TO STAND UP AGAINST THIS CRUEL SYSTEM!
STAY LOW FOR A WHILE, BHAGAT. ONE DAY, WE WILL SHOW THEM THAT WE ARE SOCIALISTS, NOT KILLERS LIKE EVERYBODY BELIEVES. SUKHDEV IS ON HIS WAY. LET HIM COME FIRST.

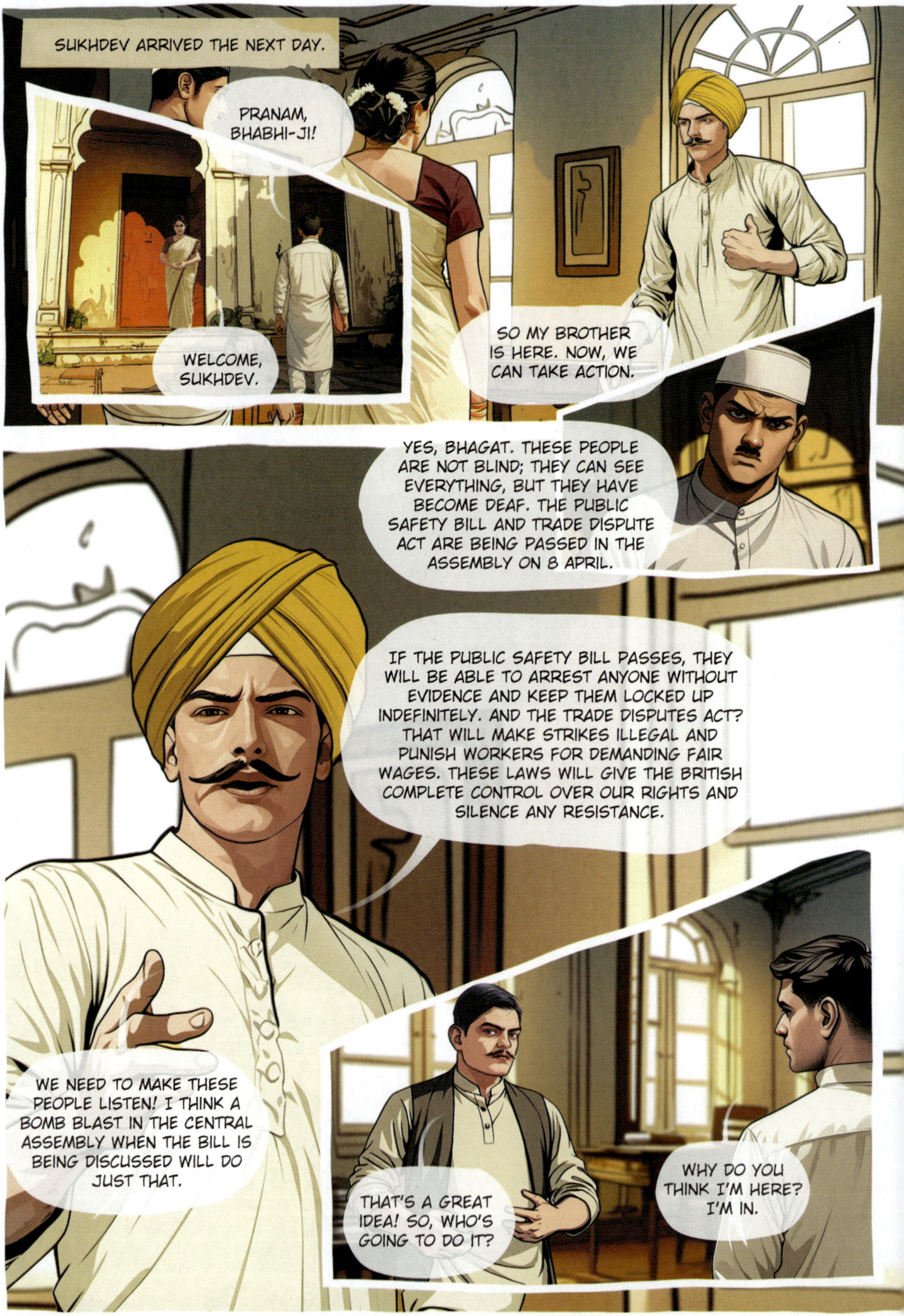
SUKHDEV ARRIVED THE NEXT DAY.
PRANAM, BHABHI-JI!
WELCOME, SUKHDEV.
SO MY BROTHER IS HERE. NOW, WE CAN TAKE ACTION.
YES, BHAGAT. THESE PEOPLE ARE NOT BLIND; THEY CAN SEE EVERYTHING, BUT THEY HAVE BECOME DEAF. THE PUBLIC SAFETY BILL AND TRADE DISPUTE ACT ARE BEING PASSED IN THE ASSEMBLY ON 8 APRIL.
IF THE PUBLIC SAFETY BILL PASSES, THEY WILL BE ABLE TO ARREST ANYONE WITHOUT EVIDENCE AND KEEP THEM LOCKED UP INDEFINITELY. AND THE TRADE DISPUTES ACT? THAT WILL MAKE STRIKES ILLEGAL AND PUNISH WORKERS FOR DEMANDING FAIR WAGES. THESE LAWS WILL GIVE THE BRITISH COMPLETE CONTROL OVER OUR RIGHTS AND SILENCE ANY RESISTANCE.
WE NEED TO MAKE THESE PEOPLE LISTEN! I THINK A BOMB BLAST IN THE CENTRAL ASSEMBLY WHEN THE BILL IS BEING DISCUSSED WILL DO JUST THAT.
THAT'S A GREAT IDEA! SO, WHO'S GOING TO DO IT?
WHY DO YOU THINK I'M HERE? I'M IN.

BHAGAT, YOU AND BATUKESHWAR DUTT WILL BE THE ONES TO DO IT.
AND THIS TIME, WE WON'T RUN. WE'LL SURRENDER.
NO BHAGAT, DON'T DO THAT. THIS IS A ONE WAY FIGHT. IF WE SURRENDER, THERE WILL BE NO COURT PROCEEDINGS OR TRIALS ... YOU COULD BE HANGED.
WHO FEARS DEATH? IF WE SURRENDER, I CAN USE THE COURTROOM AND THE MEDIA TO SEND OUR MESSAGE. I'LL SHOW EVERYONE THAT WE ARE NOT JUST KILLERS.
LONG LIVE THE REVOLUTION! DOWN WITH IMPERIALISM!
BUT HOW ARE WE GOING TO MAKE THE BOMBS?
I KNOW A CHEMISTRY PROFESSOR— JATIN DAS.
HE TRULY WANTS TO HELP US AND HE UNDERSTANDS THE RISKS. HE WILL ARRANGE ALL THE MATERIALS AND TEACH US.

GOOD JOB, BHAGAT. GHOSH, IS YOUR BOMB READY?
YES. LET'S TEST THEM OUT ON AN OPEN GROUND.
LONG LIVE THE REVOLUTION!
NOW, IT'S TIME FOR ACTION.
A WEEK BEFORE THE BOMBING IN DELHI, BHAGAT SINGH AND BATUKESHWAR DUTT STOOD OUTSIDE RAMNATH'S PHOTOGRAPHY STUDIO, PREPARING FOR THEIR BOLD ACT OF PROTEST.
LET'S PHOTOGRAPH OURSELVES. THIS TIME, WE WON'T HIDE. WE'LL SHOW OUR FACES TO THE COUNTRY ALONG WITH OUR MESSAGE.
I HAVE A FRIEND WHO WORKS IN THE ASSEMBLY. HE'S GETTING US ENTRY PASSES.
GOOD WORK, DUTT. LET'S GO SCOUT THE PLACE AND FINALISE OUR PLAN.

INSIDE THE CENTRAL LEGISLATIVE ASSEMBLY ...
THIS IS WHERE WE'LL SIT IN THE GALLERY.
AND WE'LL THROW THE BOMBS THERE. WE'LL MAKE SURE NO ONE GETS HURT.
8 APRIL 1929—THE CENTRAL LEGISLATIVE ASSEMBLY WAS IN SESSION. PRESIDENT OF THE ASSEMBLY, MR VITHALBHAI PATEL, PRESIDED OVER THE DEBATE.
LET'S SIT. STAY READY.
THE LAWMAKERS DEBATED THE PUBLIC SAFETY BILL, WHICH THREATENED TO CURB CIVIL LIBERTIES.
I AM SURE WE ALL UNDERSTAND THAT THIS BILL IS NECESSARY TO MAINTAIN LAW AND ORDER!

IT'S TIME.
DUTT IMMEDIATELY STOOD UP AND THREW THE FIRST BOMB TOWARDS AN EMPTY SECTION OF THE ASSEMBLY FLOOR.
LONG LIVE THE REVOLUTION!
DOWN WITH IMPERIALISM!
BANG

AMID THE SMOKE AND CONFUSION, BHAGAT SINGH AND DUTT THREW PAMPHLETS INTO THE AIR.
LONG LIVE THE REVOLUTION! DOWN WITH IMPERIALISM!
A loud noise is needed to make the deaf listen!
THE ASSEMBLY DESCENDED INTO CHAOS. EVERYONE PANICKED.
OH MY GOD! WHO ARE THESE PEOPLE?
HELP! I CAN'T SEE ANYTHING!
WHO ARE THESE MEN? ARREST THEM IMMEDIATELY, BEFORE THEY RUN AWAY!
WE ARE NOT RUNNING. WE SURRENDER OURSELVES WILLINGLY. HERE, TAKE MY REVOLVER.
THE PRICE OF SEEKING JUSTICE IS STEEP AND THE FINAL RECKONING COMES IN THE FORM OF A TRIAL.

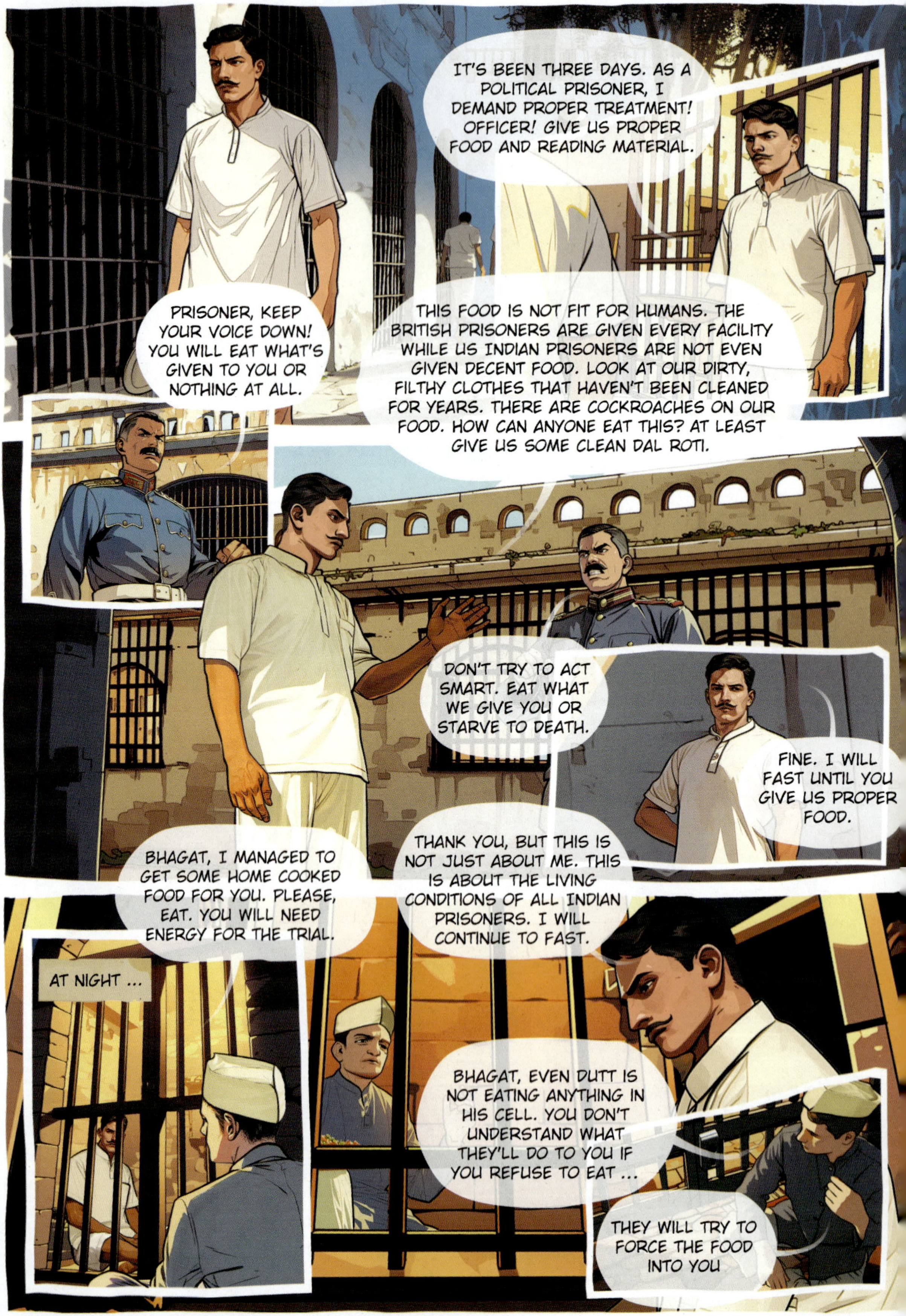
IT'S BEEN THREE DAYS. AS A POLITICAL PRISONER, I DEMAND PROPER TREATMENT! OFFICER! GIVE US PROPER FOOD AND READING MATERIAL.
PRISONER, KEEP YOUR VOICE DOWN! YOU WILL EAT WHAT'S GIVEN TO YOU OR NOTHING AT ALL.
THIS FOOD IS NOT FIT FOR HUMANS. THE BRITISH PRISONERS ARE GIVEN EVERY FACILITY WHILE US INDIAN PRISONERS ARE NOT EVEN GIVEN DECENT FOOD. LOOK AT OUR DIRTY, FILTHY CLOTHES THAT HAVEN'T BEEN CLEANED FOR YEARS. THERE ARE COCKROACHES ON OUR FOOD. HOW CAN ANYONE EAT THIS? AT LEAST GIVE US SOME CLEAN DAL ROTI.
DON'T TRY TO ACT SMART. EAT WHAT WE GIVE YOU OR STARVE TO DEATH.
FINE. I WILL FAST UNTIL YOU GIVE US PROPER FOOD.
AT NIGHT ...
BHAGAT, I MANAGED TO GET SOME HOME COOKED FOOD FOR YOU. PLEASE, EAT. YOU WILL NEED ENERGY FOR THE TRIAL.
THANK YOU, BUT THIS IS NOT JUST ABOUT ME. THIS IS ABOUT THE LIVING CONDITIONS OF ALL INDIAN PRISONERS. I WILL CONTINUE TO FAST.
BHAGAT, EVEN DUTT IS NOT EATING ANYTHING IN HIS CELL. YOU DON'T UNDERSTAND WHAT THEY'LL DO TO YOU IF YOU REFUSE TO EAT ...
THEY WILL TRY TO FORCE THE FOOD INTO YOU

TO FORCE BHAGAT TO BREAK HIS FAST, THE POLICEMEN BEAT HIM CRUELLY.
YOUR DEMANDS WILL NEVER BE MET. WE WILL DO WHATEVER IT TAKES TO BREAK YOUR HUNGER STRIKE. TOMORROW IS THE FIRST DAY OF YOUR CASE. EAT THE FOOD!
NO, UNTIL MY DEMANDS ARE MET.

THE NEXT DAY BHAHAT SINGH AND HIS COMRADES WERE BROUGHT TO THE COURT.
INQUILAB ZINDABAD!
INQUILAB ZINDABAD!
HE WAS TOUCHED TO SEE HUNDREDS OF SUPPORTERS WAITING OUTSIDE THE COURT.
WE HAVE A LOT OF SUPPORT. THIS TRIAL WILL HELP US GET OUR MESSAGE OUT TO THE PUBLIC. EVERYTHING WE WANT TO CONVEY TO THE WORLD SHALL BE SAID AND SHARED IN THIS TRIAL.

BHAGAT SINGH, YOU STAND ACCUSED OF CONSPIRACY TO MURDER, THE KILLING OF JOHN SAUNDERS AND A SERIES OF ATTACKS ON BRITISH OFFICIALS. HOW DO YOU PLEAD?
I PLEAD GUILTY TO NO CRIME EXCEPT LOVE FOR MY COUNTRY. INQUILAB ZINDABAD!
WHAT DOES INQUILAB EVEN MEAN?
IT IS A WAR CRY AGAINST TYRANNY AND INJUSTICE!
IT IS A CALL TO UNITE THE YOUTH OF INDIA.
IT IS A WEAPON AGAINST EXPLOITATION.
IT IS A WAKE UP CALL FOR THE MASSES.
ORDER! ORDER! THE LAHORE CONSPIRACY CASE CONTINUES.
YOUR HONOUR, I WANT PERMISSION TO BRING GOVERNMENT WITNESS, MR PHANINDRA NATH GHOSH TO THE WITNESS BOX.
PERMISSION GRANTED.

MR GHOSH, IS IT TRUE THAT AN ILLEGAL BOMB-MAKING FACTORY WAS ESTABLISHED BY THIS GROUP OF INDIVIDUALS? AND THAT IT WAS THOSE BOMBS THEY THREW IN THE ASSEMBLY?
YES, THEY DID.
YOU ARE A TRAITOR. YOU SOLD YOUR SOUL FOR MONEY.
YOU SON OF DHRITARASHTRA, LOOK ME IN THE EYE!
ARE THEY OFFERING YOU A JOB AND HOUSE IN ENGLAND?
SIR, WE DON'T KNOW HIM OR HOW TO MAKE BOMBS! IT IS A SOPHISTICATED TECHNIQUE. JUST LOOK AT HIM—DO YOU REALLY THINK HE KNOWS ANYTHING ABOUT MAKING A BOMB?
WHAT ARE YOU TALKING ABOUT? I CAN MAKE ANY KIND OF BOMB.
I DON'T THINK YOU KNOW EVEN A SINGLE MATERIAL USED TO MAKE A BOMB.
NO, NO, I CAN TELL YOU EVERYTHING IN DETAIL.
THEN PLEASE TELL THE COURT, MR GHOSH.

LET ME TELL YOU THE FULL LIST. YOU NEED GUN COTTON, GAUZE WIRE, AMMONIUM CARBONATE, SULPHUR, RED PHOSPHORUS, RED SULPHIDE, CARBONIC ACID, NITRIC ACID AND SULPHURIC ACID.
I HOPE YOU DIDN'T MISS ANYTHING.
BEFORE ANYONE COULD RESPOND, THE JOURNALISTS WHO HAD NOTED EVERYTHING GHOSH SAID WALKED OUT.

THANK YOU, MR GHOSH. YOU HAVE REVEALED THE MATERIALS NEEDED TO MAKE A BOMB TO EVERYONE. NOW EVERY CHILD IN INDIA CAN MAKE BOMBS BY READING TOMORROW'S NEWSPAPER.
THERE WILL NOT JUST BE ONE BHAGAT SINGH, BUT MANY BHAGAT SINGH'S APPEARING IN PLACES THAT THE BRITISH GOVERNMENT CANNOT EVEN IMAGINE.
LONG LIVE THE REVOLUTION! DOWN WITH IMPERIALISM!
OH NO! WHAT HAVE I DONE BY ASKING GHOSH TO REVEAL EVERYTHING? STOP THOSE JOURNALISTS!

THE NEWS OF WHAT HAPPENED AT COURT REACHED CHANDRASHEKAR AZAD.
WHAT AN AMAZING MOVE BY BHAGAT! WHAT A GREAT IDEA!
DADA, THE BRITISHERS ARE SO ANGRY AT HOW THEY WERE FOOLED COMPLETELY!
YES, THEY MADE SUCH A FOOL OF THE LAWYERS!
BHAGAT SINGH'S FIGHT HAPPENED NOT ONLY AT THE TRIAL BUT ALSO IN THE FORM OF A HUNGER STRIKE BACK IN JAIL. THIS SENT RIPPLES ACROSS THE EMPIRE.
IT HAS BEEN TWENTY-SIX DAYS SINCE HE STARTED HIS HUNGER STRIKE.
THIS IS JUST A PUBLICITY STUNT. DON'T WORRY, HIS POPULARITY IS NOT THE SAME AS GANDHI'S. NO ONE CARES IF HE GOES ON HUNGER STRIKE.
I STILL THINK WE SHOULD PUT A STOP TO THIS. LET'S TALK TO THE JAILOR IN LAHORE.
OPEN YOUR MOUTH! EAT, OR WE WILL BEAT YOU LIKE PIGS.
AS PER THEIR ORDERS, THE POLICE BRUTALLY PUNISHED BHAGAT AND HIS FRIENDS AND FORCED THEM TO EAT FOOD, BUT THEY DID NOT YIELD.

THE NEWS OF THE HUNGER STRIKE HAD EVEN REACHED THE VICEROY PALACE.
WHO IS THIS BHAGAT SINGH THAT EVERYONE IS TALKING ABOUT?
IT HAS BEEN FIFTY-FIVE DAYS SINCE BHAGAT SINGH AND HIS FRIENDS HAVE EATEN.
DAYS PASSED AND BHAGAT SINGH'S HUNGER STRIKE CONTINUED TO WAKE UP THE MASSES.
EAT, BETA.
NO, MA. MY FRIENDS AND I ARE FASTING IN SUPPORT OF BHAGAT SINGH'S DEMANDS FOR EQUAL TREATMENT.
IT HAD NOW BEEN SIXTY-SIX DAYS SINCE THE START OF THE HUNGER STRIKE AND JATIN DAS FELL FATALLY ILL.
HE IS NOT EVEN TAKING HIS MEDICINE. JATIN WILL NOT SURVIVE.
JATIN, PLEASE TAKE YOUR MEDICINE. THE GOVERNMENT HAS AGREED TO OUR DEMANDS.
NO, BHAGAT. I KNOW YOU ARE LYING TO MAKE ME TAKE THE MEDICINE. BUT I WILL HONOUR MY COMMITMENT. I WILL NOT BREAK. NOT UNTIL MY LAST BREATH.
LONG LIVE THE REVOLUTION!
JATIN DAS LIVES FOREVER!

JATIN DAS'S UNTIMELY DEMISE DURING THE STRIKE FURTHER INTENSIFIED PUBLIC OUTRAGE.
HOW IS THAT POSSIBLE? WE HAVE SO MANY WITNESSES IN THIS CASE.
SIR, EVEN CONGRESS IS DEMANDING TOTAL INDEPENDENCE. THE YOUTH ARE BEING INFLUENCED BY BHAGAT SINGH'S IDEOLOGIES.
SIR, BHAGAT SINGH IS USING THE COURT AS A PROPAGANDA OFFICE.
ON EVERY DATE, HE MAKES A REVOLUTIONARY SPEECH THAT THE MEDIA CAPTURES AND MOTIVATES THE YOUTH EVEN MORE.
THERE CAN BE NO DIALOGUE OR NEGOTIATION WITH THE BRITISH. ONLY WHEN THE BRITISH LEAVE INDIA CAN WE HAVE A DIALOGUE.
WE DON'T WANT DOMINION STATUS. WE WANT TOTAL INDEPENDENCE. THAT IS OUR RIGHT!
INQUILAB ZINDABAD!
SIR, YOU MUST DECLARE AN EMERGENCY AND PASS A NEW ORDINANCE SO THAT THE TRIAL CAN MOVE FORWARD WITHOUT BHAGAT SINGH'S PRESENCE. THAT WAY HE CAN BE GIVEN CAPITAL PUNISHMENT AS SOON AS POSSIBLE.

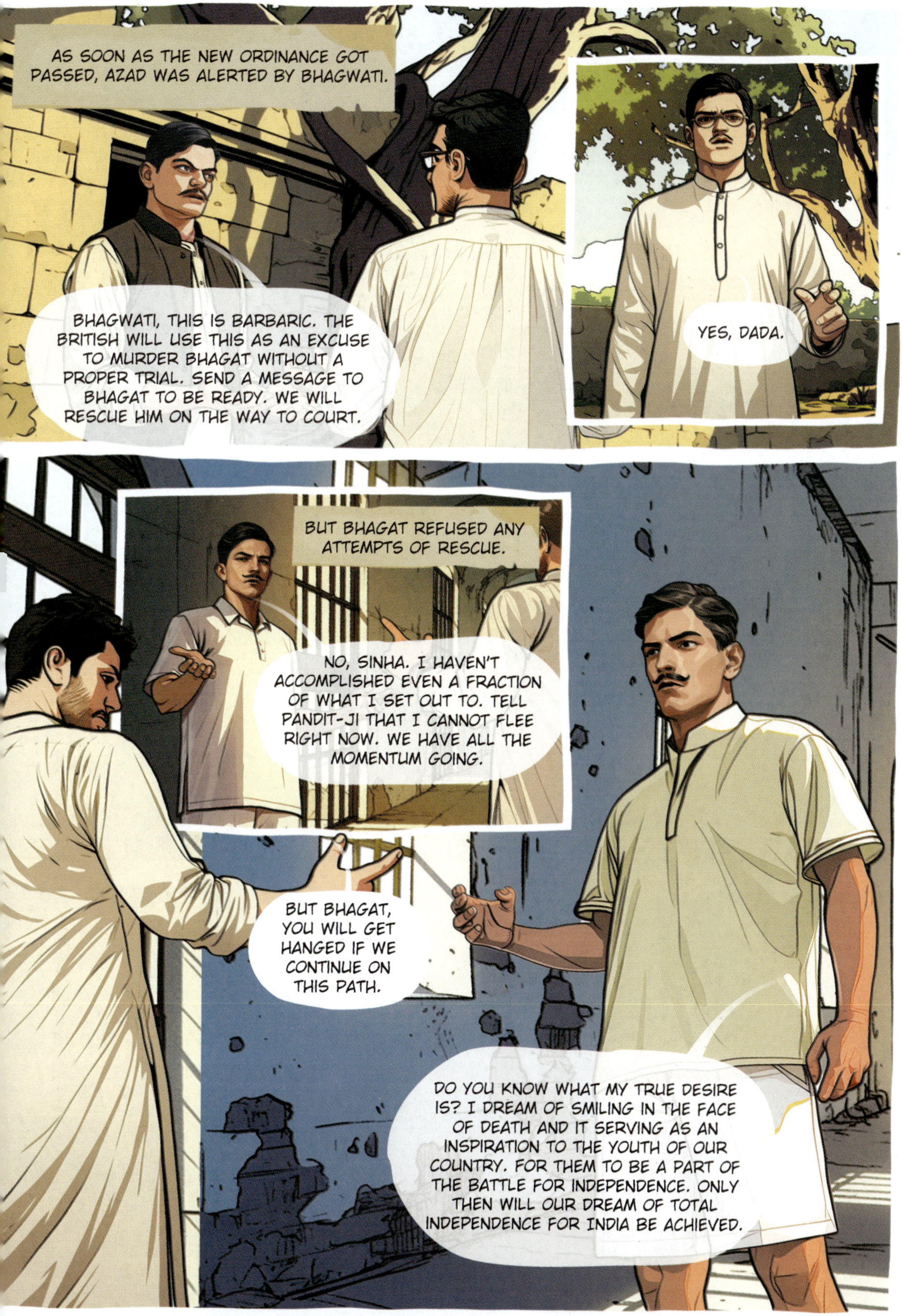
AS SOON AS THE NEW ORDINANCE GOT PASSED, AZAD WAS ALERTED BY BHAGWATI.
BHAGWATI, THIS IS BARBARIC. THE BRITISH WILL USE THIS AS AN EXCUSE TO MURDER BHAGAT WITHOUT A PROPER TRIAL. SEND A MESSAGE TO BHAGAT TO BE READY. WE WILL RESCUE HIM ON THE WAY TO COURT.
YES, DADA.
BUT BHAGAT REFUSED ANY ATTEMPTS OF RESCUE.
NO, SINHA. I HAVEN'T ACCOMPLISHED EVEN A FRACTION OF WHAT I SET OUT TO. TELL PANDIT-JI THAT I CANNOT FLEE RIGHT NOW. WE HAVE ALL THE MOMENTUM GOING.
BUT BHAGAT, YOU WILL GET HANGED IF WE CONTINUE ON THIS PATH.
DO YOU KNOW WHAT MY TRUE DESIRE IS? I DREAM OF SMILING IN THE FACE OF DEATH AND IT SERVING AS AN INSPIRATION TO THE YOUTH OF OUR COUNTRY. FOR THEM TO BE A PART OF THE BATTLE FOR INDEPENDENCE. ONLY THEN WILL OUR DREAM OF TOTAL INDEPENDENCE FOR INDIA BE ACHIEVED.

AT BHAGAT SINGH'S NEXT HEARING. THE COURT WAS STRICTER. THERE WERE NOW THREE JUDGES SITTING AT THE COURT HEARING.
WE HAVE TRIED EVERY POSSIBLE WAY TO BE HEARD. WE BEGAN WITH PEACEFUL PROTESTS BUT OFFICERS LIKE GENERAL DYER, J. SCOTT AND OTHER BRITISH OFFICIALS MASSACRED THOUSANDS OF INNOCENT PEOPLE.
THE ASSEMBLY MEMBERS FAILED TO HEAR OUR CRIES. IT WAS TO AWAKEN THEM TO THE CRUELTY OF THIS SYSTEM THAT WE TOOK DRASTIC ACTION BY SETTING OFF A BOMB. WE DO NOT WANT THESE OPPRESSIVE BILLS TO BE PASSED BY THE BRITISH GOVERNMENT. WE DEMAND FULL INDEPENDENCE AND ARE READY TO SACRIFICE EVERYTHING FOR IT.
LONG LIVE THE REVOLUTION! DOWN WITH IMPERIALISM!
ORDER! ORDER!

THIS IS OUR COUNTRY, OUR MOTHERLAND AND IT IS OUR BIRTHRIGHT TO LIVE HERE IN FREEDOM. REMEMBER THE JALLIANWALA BAGH MASSACRE—WHAT WAS THEIR CRIME?
WHAT WAS THE FAULT OF OUR BELOVED LALA LAJPAT RAI? WAS IT SIMPLY FIGHTING FOR FREEDOM?
THEY ALL BELIEVED IN NON-VIOLENCE AND PEACEFUL PROTESTS, YET WHAT DID THEY RECEIVE IN RETURN?
I JUST WANT TO SAY THAT THERE IS NOTHING WRONG IN DEMANDING YOUR BIRTHRIGHT—YOUR FREEDOM. IF WE CANNOT ACHIEVE IT PEACEFULLY, THEN THERE IS ONLY ONE PATH LEFT—REVOLUTION! WE DEMAND NOTHING LESS THAN FULL INDEPENDENCE!
BHAGAT SINGH, WE ARE WITH YOU!
LONG LIVE THE REVOLUTION! DOWN WITH IMPERIALISM!

JAWAHARLAL NEHRU
MAHATMA GANDHI
BHAGAT SINGH'S IDEAS ARE EVERYWHERE, BAPU. HE IS JUST TWENTY-TWO AND HIS MESSAGE OF FULL INDEPENDENCE RESONATES EVEN WITH OUR YOUNG CONGRESS LEADERS.
VIOLENCE IS NOT OUR PATH, NEHRU. IT'S NOT WHO WE ARE. I DON'T SUPPORT HIS THOUGHTS.
AS BHAGAT SINGH'S WORDS ECHOED THROUGH THE HEARTS OF THE YOUTH OF INDIA, HIS CALL FOR 'INQUILAB ZINDABAD' STIRRED A WAVE OF REVOLUTION. HIS MESSAGE REACHED FAR BEYOND THE WALLS OF THE COURTROOM, FINDING ITS WAY INTO THE QUIET DISCUSSIONS OF THE CONGRESS LEADERSHIP.
HE IS BECOMING EVEN MORE POPULAR THAN GANDHI. THIS MAN HOLDS THE POWER OF THOUSANDS OF REVOLUTIONARIES. THERE'S ONLY ONE WAY TO STOP HIM NOW. BRING THE WITNESSES AND WRAP UP THE TRIAL AS FAST AS POSSIBLE.
OKAY, SIR.
THE NEXT DAY AT COURT ...
OUR FIRST WITNESS IS HERE, MR RAM SARAN DAS. WE HAVE HIS SIGNED TESTIMONY ...
THAT TESTIMONY IS A LIE. I WAS TORTURED AND FORCED TO SIGN IT.
INQUILAB ...
... ZINDABAD!

YOUR HONOUR, NEXT I WANT TO CALL MR JAI GOPAL TO THE STAND.
THIS TRIBUNAL SYSTEM IS ILLEGAL. ALL THE WITNESSES YOU HAVE PRESENTED ARE FAKE. WHAT IS THE POINT OF THIS CHARADE?
SO, MR. JAI GOPAL, DO YOU ADMIT THAT THESE PEOPLE ARE RESPONSIBLE FOR SAUNDERS' MURDER?
YES, SIR. I WAS ALSO A PART OF THE MURDER.

SUKHDEV PLANNED EVERYTHING AND RAJGURU AND BHAGAT SINGH EXECUTED THE MURDER.
YOU TRAITOR!
YOUR HONOUR, THIS IS CONTEMPT OF COURT! HANDCUFF THEM!
YOUR HONOUR, I APOLOGISE FOR MY FRIEND'S BEHAVIOUR. BUT THIS IS A COURT OF LAW. THE HANDCUFFS SHOULD NOT BE USED INSIDE.

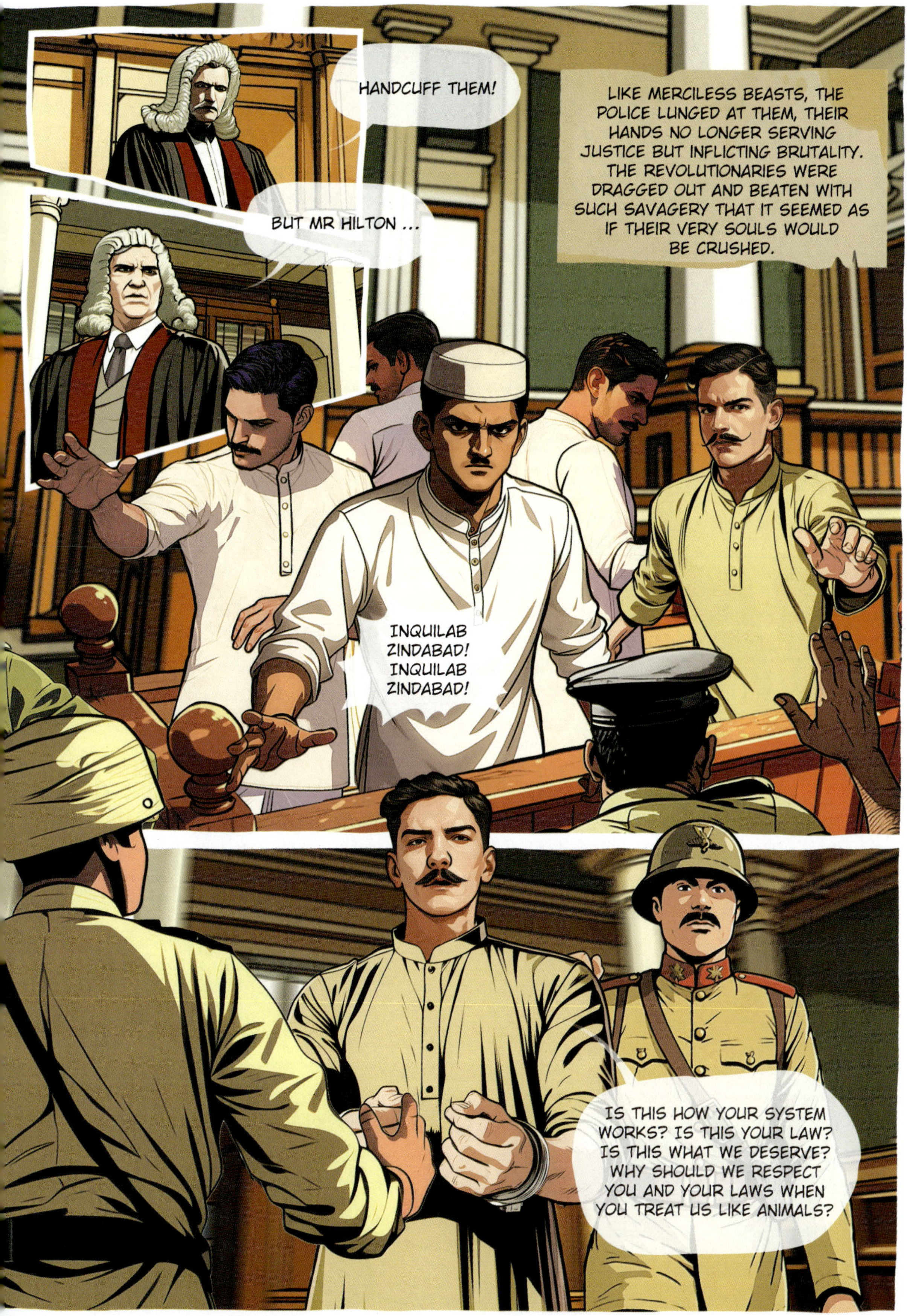
HANDCUFF THEM!
BUT MR HILTON ...
LIKE MERCILESS BEASTS, THE POLICE LUNGED AT THEM, THEIR HANDS NO LONGER SERVING JUSTICE BUT INFLICTING BRUTALITY. THE REVOLUTIONARIES WERE DRAGGED OUT AND BEATEN WITH SUCH SAVAGERY THAT IT SEEMED AS IF THEIR VERY SOULS WOULD BE CRUSHED.
INQUILAB ZINDABAD! INQUILAB ZINDABAD!
IS THIS HOW YOUR SYSTEM WORKS? IS THIS YOUR LAW? IS THIS WHAT WE DESERVE? WHY SHOULD WE RESPECT YOU AND YOUR LAWS WHEN YOU TREAT US LIKE ANIMALS?

ORDER! ORDER!
I WON'T STEP FOOT IN THAT COURT AGAIN! WHAT IS THE POINT OF A PLACE WHERE JUSTICE IS NOTHING BUT A JOKE AND THE TRUTH IS BURIED UNDER LIES. I REFUSE TO BE A PART OF THIS MOCKERY! YOU MAY ANNOUNCE YOUR PRE-DESTINED VERDICT WHENEVER YOU WISH.
AND SO THE COURT ANNOUNCED ITS VERDICT THE NEXT DAY ON 7 OCTOBER 1930.
AFTER TAKING INTO ACCOUNT ALL THE EVIDENCE AND ARGUMENTS, THE TRIBUNAL PRONOUNCES THE FOLLOWING SENTENCES IN THE LAHORE CONSPIRACY CASE. BEJOY KUMAR SINHA, KISHORILAL, MAHAVEER SINGH, SHIV VERMA, GAYA PRASAD, JAIDEV AND KAMALNATH TIWARI—TRANSPORTATION FOR LIFE.
RAJGURU—UNDER SECTION 121 AND 302, DEATH BY HANGING. SUKHDEV—UNDER SECTION 121 AND 302, DEATH BY HANGING. BHAGAT SINGH—UNDER SECTION 121 AND 302, DEATH BY HANGING. ALL THREE TO BE HANGED BY THE NECK UNTIL THEY ARE DEAD.

THE NEWS WAS CONVEYED TO BHAGAT SINGH AND HIS FRIENDS.
THANK YOU VERY MUCH! LONG LIVE THE REVOLUTION!
TAKE THEM TO THE CONDEMNED CELLS TILL THE DAY OF THEIR DEATH.
BHAGAT SINGH ZINDABAAD! SUKHDEV ZINDAABAD! RAJGURU ZINDABAAD!

WITH EACH PASSING DAY, THE POLICE GREW MORE VIGILANT. THEIR EYES WERE NOW FIXED ON CHANDRASHEKHAR AZAD.
27 FEBRUARY 1931, ALFRED PARK, ALLAHABAD.
PANDIT-JI, WHY DON'T YOU ESCAPE TO RUSSIA?
NO. I WILL NOT ABANDON THE FIGHT FOR OUR LAND. PLEASE TAKE THIS MONEY AND GIVE IT TO RAGURU'S MOTHER. SHE NEEDS IT.
WHAT WILL BE OUR NEXT MOVE?
NOW WE MUST PLOT TO GET BHAGAT SINGH, RAJGURU AND SUKHDEV FREE BEFORE THEIR HANGING.
PANDIT-JI, I TAKE YOUR LEAVE NOW. I MUST GO TO RECEIVE MY SISTER AT THE STATION.
OKAY, VEERBHADRA.

BUT VEERBHADRA HAD OTHER PLANS.
HE IS INSIDE. HE CAN BE EASILY SHOT.
THE POLICE TOOK AIM AND SHOT AZAD IN HIS LEG.
BANG!
AH! WE HAVE BEEN BETRAYED! RAJ, RUN! DON'T WORRY ABOUT ME.
THE POLICE SURROUNDED AZAD FROM ALL SIDES.
BANG!
AZAD FOUGHT FEROCIOUSLY ...

... BUT HE WAS OUTNUMBERED.
FORGIVE ME, MOTHER. I CAN'T SERVE YOU ANY LONGER.
VANDE MATRAM!
BOOM!

THE ENTIRE COUNTRY WAS NOW UNITED UNDER ONE SLOGAN—TO COMMUTE THE SENTENCES OF BHAGAT SINGH, SUKHDEV AND RAJGURU.
THE COUNTRY DEMANDS THAT THE HANGINGS OF BHAGAT SINGH, SUKHDEV AND RAJGURU MUST BE PARDONED. BHAGAT SINGH IS NOT JUST A NAME. HE IS A MOVEMENT.
SUBHAS CHANDRA BOSE
HIS PATRIOTISM IS INSPIRING.
SAVE CO
BHAGAT SINGH, RAJ
LONG LIVE BHAGAT SINGH!

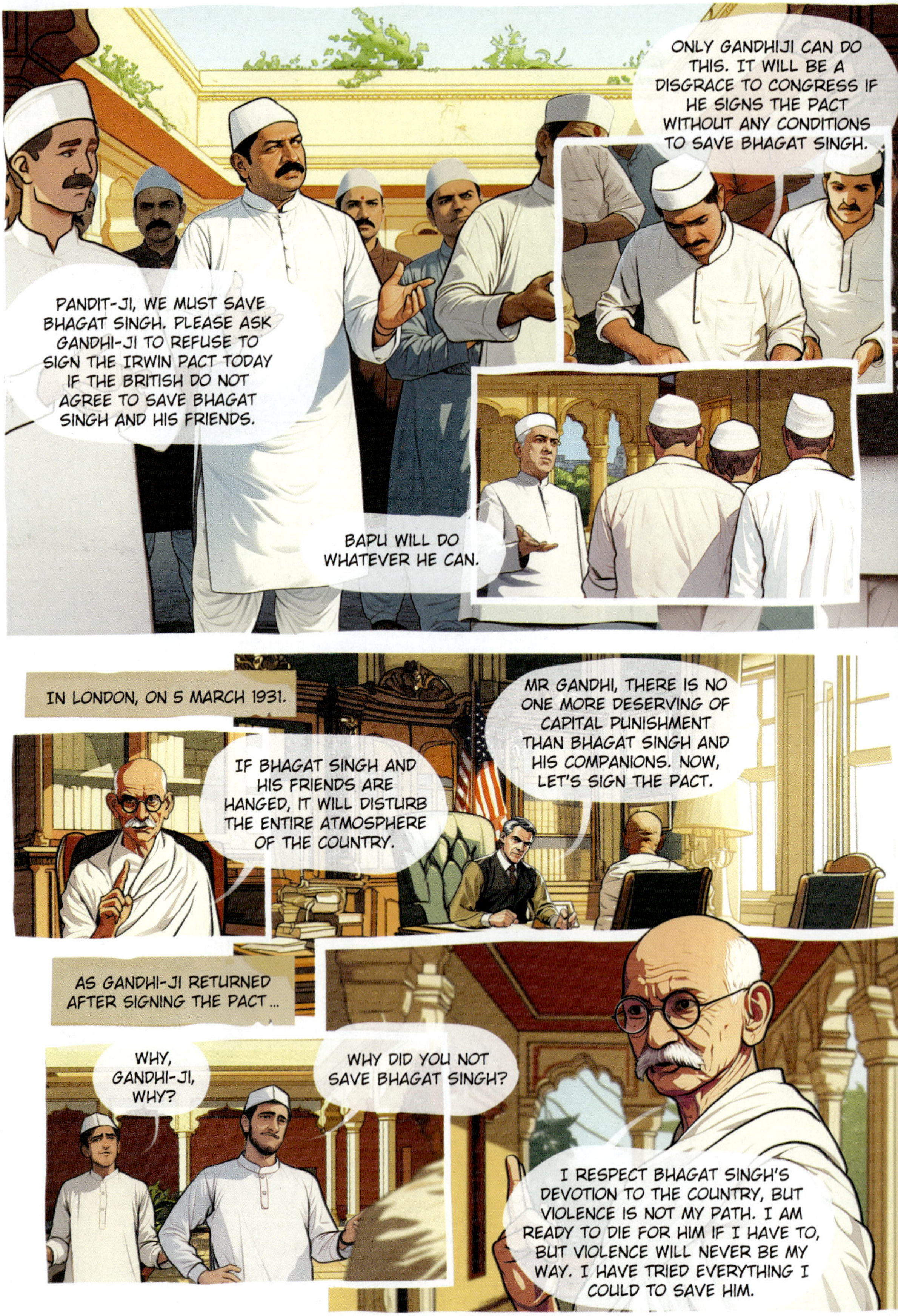
PANDIT-JI, WE MUST SAVE BHAGAT SINGH. PLEASE ASK GANDHI-JI TO REFUSE TO SIGN THE IRWIN PACT TODAY IF THE BRITISH DO NOT AGREE TO SAVE BHAGAT SINGH AND HIS FRIENDS.
ONLY GANDHIJI CAN DO THIS. IT WILL BE A DISGRACE TO CONGRESS IF HE SIGNS THE PACT WITHOUT ANY CONDITIONS TO SAVE BHAGAT SINGH.
BAPU WILL DO WHATEVER HE CAN.
IN LONDON, ON 5 MARCH 1931.
IF BHAGAT SINGH AND HIS FRIENDS ARE HANGED, IT WILL DISTURB THE ENTIRE ATMOSPHERE OF THE COUNTRY.
MR GANDHI, THERE IS NO ONE MORE DESERVING OF CAPITAL PUNISHMENT THAN BHAGAT SINGH AND HIS COMPANIONS. NOW, LET'S SIGN THE PACT.
AS GANDHI-JI RETURNED AFTER SIGNING THE PACT...
WHY, GANDHI-JI, WHY?
WHY DID YOU NOT SAVE BHAGAT SINGH?
I RESPECT BHAGAT SINGH'S DEVOTION TO THE COUNTRY, BUT VIOLENCE IS NOT MY PATH. I AM READY TO DIE FOR HIM IF I HAVE TO, BUT VIOLENCE WILL NEVER BE MY WAY. I HAVE TRIED EVERYTHING I COULD TO SAVE HIM.

IN JAIL, 23 MARCH 1931.
PREPARE FOR THE HANGINGS OF BHAGAT SINGH, SUKHDEV AND RAJGURU.
RIGHT NOW, SIR? ISN'T IT TOMORROW?
THERE ARE FRESH ORDERS.
BUT WHY?
THE SITUATION IS BECOMING MORE VOLATILE BY THE DAY. WITH PROTESTS INTENSIFYING AND THE NATION RALLYING BEHIND BHAGAT SINGH, IT HAS BEEN DECIDED THAT WE CAN'T AFFORD ANY MORE DELAY. THE EXECUTION MUST BE CARRIED OUT TODAY, BEFORE PRESSURE FROM THE MASSES FORCES US TO RECONSIDER.
MY FRIENDS, THE DECISION HAS BEEN MADE. THE DAY HAS FINALLY COME! I'M EXCITED TO MEET LENIN THE REVOLUTIONARY!

SIR, SHOULDN'T WE HANDCUFF THEM?
NOT TODAY.
RAJGURU, WHAT ARE YOUR LAST WORDS?
JUST TELL THE WARDEN TO COLLECT THE CARROM BOARD AND BOOKS. THAT'S ALL.
WE WILL COME BACK AGAIN TO SERVE OUR NATION.

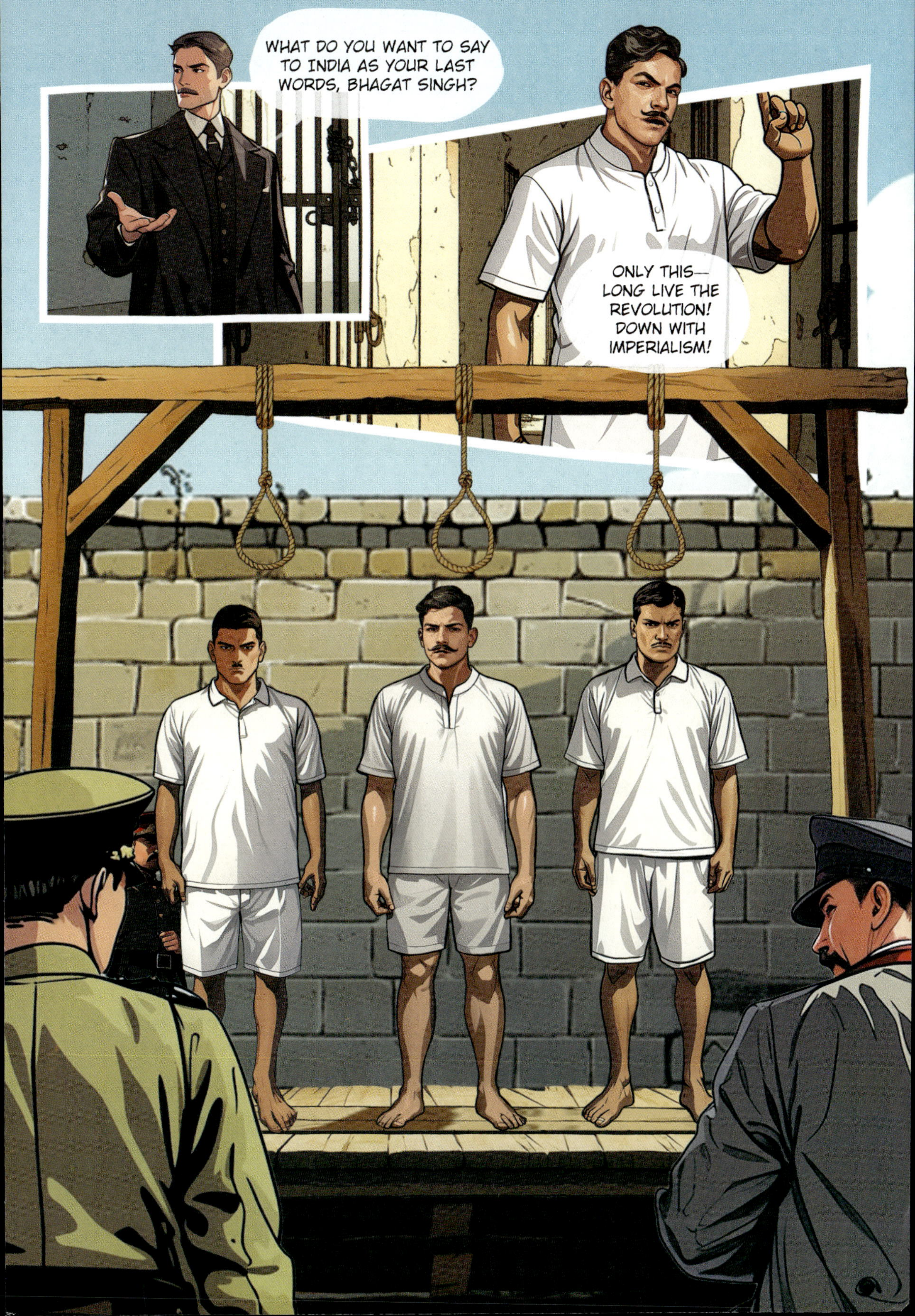
WHAT DO YOU WANT TO SAY TO INDIA AS YOUR LAST WORDS, BHAGAT SINGH?
ONLY THIS— LONG LIVE THE REVOLUTION! DOWN WITH IMPERIALISM!

ANY LAST WISHES?
WE JUST WANT TO HUG FOR THE LAST TIME. THAT'S ALL.
INQUILAB ZINDABAD!
AT THE GALLOWS, THREE BRAVE SOULS STOOD DEFIANT, THEIR LIVES SACRIFICED FOR THE FREEDOM OF A NATION THAT WOULD NEVER FORGET THEIR COURAGE.

THE NEWS SPREAD LIKE WILDFIRE—THE MARTYRDOM OF BHAGAT SINGH, SUKHDEV AND RAJGURU WAS A BLOW THAT WOULD SHAKE THE VERY CORE OF INDIA.
ACROSS HOMES, TEARS FLOWED—NOT JUST FOR THE LOSS OF THREE BRAVE MEN, BUT FOR THE HOPE THAT THEIR SACRIFICE WOULD NOT BE IN VAIN.
THE YOUTH, INSPIRED BY THE COURAGE OF THESE MARTYRS, ROSE WITH NEW FERVOUR, THEIR VOICES LOUDER THAN EVER IN THE FIGHT FOR INDEPENDENCE.
BHAGAT SINGH'S SACRIFICE WILL FUEL OUR REVOLUTION!
BHAGAT SINGH'S SACRIFICE DID NOT MARK THE END OF A JOURNEY, BUT THE BEGINNING OF AN UNSHAKABLE RESOLVE. HIS SPIRIT IGNITED THE HEARTS OF MILLIONS AND HIS DREAM OF A FREE INDIA LIVED ON IN EVERY PROTEST, EVERY REVOLUTION AND EVERY STEP TOWARDS INDEPENDENCE. THE BRITISH EMPIRE MAY HAVE SILENCED HIS VOICE, BUT THE ROAR OF FREEDOM GREW LOUDER, ECHOING THROUGH EVERY CORNER OF THE NATION. LONG LIVE THE REVOLUTION, FOR THE FIGHT FOR FREEDOM WAS FAR FROM OVER.